Willy-Willy

Terry Gulliver

For Lasse

I wish I were a fairy prince
And if it came to pass
I'd climb up in the rocks and trees
And slide down on my hands and knees

Contents

Prologue: Svea   v

1. Salt Lakes   1

2. Perth   16

3. Voyage to Other Worlds   34

4. Uppsala   43

5. Dalarna   82

6. The Lads   133

7. Stockholm   139

8. Epilogues   170

    Adela's letter   170

    Svea's journal   173

Glossary   180

Sources   184

Svea

Psych assessment notes by CAL, 9/10/1961
Referral by BB, Avesta Grundskola

Subject: **Svea Bergström** b 1948
Parents Bengt B, civil engineer and (?) blacksmith; Adela B, nursing administrator. One brother 4 years younger, Rolf.

Behavioral issues: According to school counsellor records, S. is *rebellious*; there are incidents of violence. It is said, possibly pubescent culmination of childhood antisocial disorder, caused by large facial birthmark. School counsellors mostly want authoritative confirmation of their pseudo-Viennese reports. Recent act provoked principal's referral.

Intimations of personality disorder seem wrong. No narcissistic displays evidenced and seems to have at least average empathy for other children, especially younger (protective?). Capable, however, of immense fierceness it seems. I think obverse of the shame common with birthmarks and such stigma. This fierceness has intimidated many, including some of her teachers. Others too; pacing panther.

Birthmark from lower right cheek to collarbone, purplish with some down. Not operable at time of birth. Direct question by me: If you could have it removed now, would you? Glare. I mean, if it were routine surgery and easy? "*No!*" The glare comes from the unmarked side; the "blaze" side of the face expresses differences which I cannot readily read (*masked* one would say). Very strong sense of two persons. Takes time to get past this and listen to the voice, which is strong, quiet, punchy, not patient. One wants film to review whether this impression—split sides—is real with some neuro dislocation or subjective. Not much chance of film. Have to observe over however many more sessions, possibly two. Interesting, glare shows not intimidated in the least by me.

Records: Father's mother in early years told her it was a mark ("blaze") of the fairy (*näck*) people, that she was special and protected. Seems to have clung to that up until perhaps age seven, but now shrugs it off. I asked: Did you once think your father was perhaps, then, not Bengt? Raise of the eyebrows; silence. No indication this even came up in old assessments, but seems she imagined fairies were farther back in the ancestry. School counsellors Freudians in all the wrong places.

One teacher noted transient strong attachment to the song *Girl in the Tree* by Sjöström* (I wonder if it is you was the little girl with blue-black hair blown out of the tallest tree in the broadest forest, etc.). She amused at my bringing it up. I pointed it out in the record. She said, "I suppose I was a child then. Do not remember it." But said, when quite young, was told by Farmor she could make a wish for an Icelandic pony, and that would settle it. If one came, she, Farmor, would care for it. Svea offered this: testing me? Asked if Farmor was still with us: regrettably not. I said would have liked to meet grandmother, on her own account and as her forbear, something about strong interesting people. Complex flickers, no message intended for me; no breakthrough; I had missed the invitation, if there was one.

Challenged: It is said you recently attacked a boy; that you lacerated his cheek and punched his nose so it bled. "*Yes.*" But what do you have to say about that? "He picked me up from behind and jeered at me. He said I was nothing to be afraid of anymore." So you showed him. "Perhaps." Did he hurt you?

"*No.*"

He was much bigger, how then? Shrugged. Explosive ferocity I am guessing. Not the first.

So why? "He wanted to be a bully. Perhaps now he will not be." To you? "To anyone." And what did the other kids say? "Do not know, did not care."

It says here you find schoolwork unchallenging and only sometimes do the work, so you scrape by. "Perhaps." Just perhaps? Looked down; avoidance, but not rebellion. Mathematics teacher advocating advanced classes to push her (and maybe get her out of his class) though only average performance; chemistry teacher says she breaks glassware; biology teacher says she will not follow the material but asks questions out of advanced class books. Unnervingly, repels their efforts to befriend (condescension). They are not sure she is savant or bitch. Strike that, of course.

Ask her next: how she feels about advanced classes. What about music, art? What about the puberty? Does she tear into boys because they are bigger? Usch. No clear vectors. Remind me why I agreed to work with teens. It is—they are—beyond me. Perhaps that is why. Between children and the psychotics.

S. reluctant to talk about family. Seems at least "normal", conscious some/most (??) stress comes from her. Expect home partly cloudy with chance of tornadoes.

Mother here Tuesday: nursing administrator. Scientific/ technical family, with child's birthmark link to fairy ancestry: compare with lit sectarian cases and witch self-identifications.

*Girl in the tree: 1955 nursery rhyme – folk song – Fritz
Sjöström (trans Gulliver)

*In the top of the highest tree
In the widest forest in the broadest land
Is a little girl with blue-black hair

And when the wind blows that tall tree
In the wide forest in that broad land
Then that mane reaches across the whole land

If one day it blows harder
In that wide wide forest in that great land
So that the tallest tree stands no more
But with a crash like a breaking string
It falls, and the blue black mane flashes and disappears;
aah!

You child listening with the blue-black hair
I wonder was it you blasted out of that tallest tree.

In the widest forest in the broadest land
On the day that tree was shattered.*

Chapter 1 Salt Lakes

1972, summer australis, vicinity of the black stump.

Willy and Bruce were following salt lake or playa perimeters by passes down old fencelines and jags along the crusty shores, with company Land Rover tires deflated to ten pounds, dodging bluish salt patches and skirting blinding white dunes of gypsum dust, looking for the gamma highs on the Bureau of Mineral Resources airborne maps. Often pulled at by soft spots, at which the driver's foot gambled between brake and accelerator. Looking for meagre shade in the mulga tree line above the lake bed to boil the billy for tea every couple of hours to keep the sweat up.

Wherever they located a gamma "hot spot" on the BMR maps, they dug a hole as deep as practical with shovels—three-four feet through crust and salt-clay slime—logged readings on one wall with a scintillometer, described the muck as if it were the geology they were trained for, and took a sample. Willy had an inkling the rare yellow specks in soft caliche might be carnotite, after poring through the weathered old *Danas Mineralogy*: uranium leached from granites and handed down in blue-moon rains along the ooze to some sort of carbonate-sulfate front. They were geologists, not geochemists, and putzing around in the slime was a bit *infra dig*, going from rock hammers to shovels to look for "New Testament" uranium, as Bruce called it ("hardly old as Moses").

Every now and then they went to a town to refuel and call in to the Perth office. There was no relief from the heat to be had in the old hotels, so they would more often find a windmill, wash in a bucket of cold water from the tank, and camp in the bush *en route* to the next map target. Perhaps every ten days they drove to Kalgoorlie and a night with an air conditioner, orange bedspreads, cigarette burns, and smells of spoiled fruit. The towns crawled with geologists, new Land Rovers and Land Cruisers bashing about in the nickel frenzy, and rooms were not always available. In midsummer there were more geologists in the survivable south, taking refuge from the insufferable heat of the north, the Pilbara. Where the temperature would not drop below one hundred Fahrenheit, even at night, for three straight months.

Half the cheesier motels had a version of the same cartoon over the counter: "Three weeks ago I didn't know how to spell geologist, now I Я one."

Once they had finished two pits on Lake Barlee, and came to the end of a fence at the shore where a small island stood just a few hundred yards out across the encrusted clay. No map gamma interest here; but Bruce idled the Land Rover a half minute while they looked across.

"So this fence just ends on the shoreline, as if the bloody sheep would not walk around the end in the crud," mused Willy.

"Well maybe they all just walked on over to the east shore, is why we haven't seen any on this station," said Bruce. "Or out to that island, Shangri La, don't it look like. Don't think we can make it out there in the Rover."

"Not so far, but fuck."

"It has a basalt ridge on the other side, and maybe a deeper slope."

"Yeah. What I am thinking too . . . would be a good spot for a comparative pit, eh? Far from runoff tribs."

"Runoff? Hasn't rained here in a century, mate."

"Would be completely tropo to try to cross the bugger, but you could walk it with couple gallons of water on your back."

"Jesus, Willy, you are giving me serious doubts about the meaning of life. But . . . "

"But?"

"Shit. It is just far enough there might be a distinct species of termite over there!"

"Looks like one of those mistakes that are dying to be made!"

"Yeah. A galloping gerund. A regular fucking brumby of a."

Bruce revved the engine.

"Wait, wait-wait!" said Willy. "You are off your bloody trolley!"

"Shit. We got the Flying Doctor," said Bruce.

"Ayup, Charlie, this is Whisky India X-ray," said Willy into his fist, "we need a tow truck with a half mile cable and a couple them levitating yogis on Lake Wotsit. Just a couple hundred miles nor-west of Kalgoorlie, mate. Over."

"Barlee. It's Lake Barlee, still, Willy. What are the tires at?"

"Up. I can let 'em down right quick. . . "

So, pretty quick, there went Bruce, double-clutching through three gears as the Rover charged on semi-flat tires across the salt crusted clay toward the island, only to settle in the muck like a goose on a pond. Willy had his door open for a quick escape, and stepped out two feet closer to the ground than getting in.

With suppressed chuckles subsiding into grimness, *why in hell did we do that, etc*, they took the axe and walked back inland to find brush and tree trunks to put under wheels. Cutting down an iron-hard mulga trunk for a winching anchor took two hours. Shite. They hauled all that material out onto the playa, lifted up one side then the other with the Handyman jack to place branches beneath the wheels, and buried the tree trunk with a cable around it thirty feet behind the vehicle.

By the time they were ready to try the first pull, the vehicle had settled soddenly back to its belly, so they jacked each side and supplemented the under-wheel filler again. They winched the vehicle eight feet before it sank off the brush fill back to its pan. Eighty to go, but it would get easier toward the shore, no? The answer actually was no—not yet at least. After the third winching the sun went down, and the work was darker, but not, it seemed, any cooler. Willy dug up the anchor tree, which had pulled nearly to the surface, and reburied it thirty feet closer to the shore.

Five billies of tea up in the trees and neither of them had pissed an ounce, or uttered more than three intelligible syllables together. Afraid the vehicle might settle steadily through the night, they persisted by starlight and the nearly full moon, then tried to gauge the settling with finger swipes on the tires at mud level while they ate canned peaches, before continuing grimly through uncertainty until sunrise. Neither uttered a word about the D-9 Cat that had gone off the end of the causeway it was building down at Kambalda, and sank out of sight through the salt muck overnight.

"Halfway!" Willy mused. "'N some blisters. Ready to give it another shot?"

"K'off."

"Well, with the axles free, we might oughta give her a trial backup."

"Dig up that anchor again first. Don't wanna sink on top of it."

"And don't bust a lay shaft with that vicious clutch slamming of yours, Bruce, when we do it."

"Lookit those fucking ruts. It's gonna last fifty years."

"You wanna fill 'em in?"

"Nah, mate. Let's leave it as a monument to mistakes needing to be made."

"Howabout just running the scintillometer along the rut and writing it up as a long trench assessing variability where the aero-gamma map is flat?"

"Eh, they'd hate and love it, the Canadians. "

"Gonna want to go to town after this Bruce?"

"Well, we're not out yet, and, no, I am kinda embarrassed to think about telling anyone about this, eh?"

"OK, enough until we get the hell out."

"I would like to keep on backing out and go back to real bloody rocks, to hell with this pestilence," said Bruce brutally.

"You don't find this interesting, mate? I think it's fascinating, just wildly fascinating, the idea of uranium hiding in this muck."

"You're about ready for the funny farm Willy!"

***

Even after reaching firm ground the next day, digging up the cable again, scraping clay and packing up took them into the late afternoon. One last walk out the track to the deep end-ruts, should be some bastard buried in them to warrant the feeling the grim reaper had been there, circling like a crow. The island, sullenly floating in the intense light, no reason whatsoever they should have thought to go there, now evil looking like a gothic fortress ruin.

"Mate, should find a tank and wash the bottom, sumpin. Then we can do a proper car wash in town."

"Yeah, I need about a dozen buckets of cold water too. 'N you look like you been at a corroboree."

"Yeah, screw logging the trench unless it beeps on a quick scan. Too late to be setting out to town today. Or trying to get far through those, those . . . endless bloody stakes along the fence. Shite, Bruce."

"Howabout this thing on the map. Not far. Dead Mans Soak, it says. Don't see any windmills closer."

So, they diverted to check out Dead Mans Soak—a dot on the quad map. As the Land Rover growled up to a treeless stretch, a dozen roos sloshed away, like drunkards from a raid on an illicit bar, and a score of black goannas ran on hind legs to splash into the hole, a blackwater eye in a caliche hollow.

"Scene of the crime, eh?" quipped Bruce.

They walked around the hole, bemused that no goanna nostrils could be seen sticking out of the blackness.

Willy noticed one tire was low, and said, "We might as well fix those spares while we have some open ground, eh?"

Another puncture getting there from the lake, spiked by iron-hard stakes of brush cut for sheep fences maybe fifty years ago, so both spares flat again: three to fix. Jesus, who thought to run sheep out here? Out with the jack, bead breaker, and tire irons. Some small vein of grim satisfaction in getting a wheel with split rim off, a hot patch on the tube, and it all back together and pumped up ready to drive on in twenty minutes. Three wheels in forty minutes. Willy boiled a billy for tea; a blaze from a handful of dry grass and twigs against the black side of the billy was enough to boil a quart of town water out of the Rover tank. Back at you, bloody sun.

"Hey, c'mere. Look at this, Bruce."

A rusty piece of iron hung on a wire across two barkless forks of a tree. Very careful lettering, punched with a nail or spike, read:

P MACK
AGED 31
KILLED BY BLACKS
14/7/94

"Well, bugger me."

Grunts and throat clearings as they shambled about, re-reading the plaque, sipping black tea, shucking lees across the red earth.

"Bloody flies are bad. Probably the roo shit trails to the soak," muttered Bruce.

"Yeah."

"When did Paddy Hannan find the Golden Mile?"

"Sometime ninety-three I reckon."

"So here they came."

"Yeah, bugger me."

The film advance in Willy's camera was stuck or broken, so he got his notebook to record the plaque. So short, and shocked onto his eyeballs as it was, he still had to read each line aloud before writing it, as flies crawled across his hands and sunglasses. Is that '94 or '96? July: shorter days, not so hot as now. Not to blame it on the sun then. Black and white, superstition and lies, mirages. Memorialized by a punctilious survivor, white. Blacks: a category of the incomprehensible.

Patrick White's *Voss* half a century earlier than Mack, Willy thought, had a comet, seen as evil omen by the blackfellers. They killed him in the same bloody desert a couple thousand miles east. I forget Voss's real name. Couple big comets in 1845. Must look up comets of 1894, for Mack. Write that. Mind faint in heat. Voss thought he might be Christ or something, blacks associated him with evils of the comet. Bugger me.

"Flies are bloody bad. Wotcher say we try to get onto that wee ridge to catch a little breeze, if we're lucky, at sunset," he said.

"Not to mention the stunning view. Think I'll have an olive in me tea tonight, eh Willy."

Camp kitchen was a folding table thirty feet off the vehicle, with the gas lantern set out to read by, or to prove later the hospitality of the local insects. For aperitifs, a can of peaches in enamel mugs.

"Think we can cook something, Willy, mate? Stuff in the cooler we oughter eat."

"Too hot. I couldn't eat. Do yourself something, if you want."

"Too . . . too."

Lurid sunset. On another shore, with an actual body of water, it might inspire a *wow*. Bruce poured a pint of water into each of the two metal pans, and they wiped faces and hands with a rag, then peeled off shirts and sponged chests, arms, and backs, at a manly distance from each another. The cooling was a whisper longer than the word "ephemeral"—a moist waft of body odor quickly evaporating, and absorbed into the aridity of quartz dust.

"Don't turn the lantern on for me. I cannot read or write."

"Nor me, but I might try the crossword. Mind needs a place to go," mumbled Bruce.

So Bruce pored over the wadded paper with lantern turned low, mumbling clues and swatting the last, slow flies away, as Willy sponged himself behind the knees and on the neck again.

"Here's a bugger of a thing. Clue is *sanguine*. Ends in *y*. I swear it is 'bloody!' I'll be go to hell, I swear it is. What is the country coming to?"

"You forget, man, since that Princess Anne said 'bloody wind' in Sydney—or was it 'bloody horse'—and the papers ran it, *bloody* is an honorable word, so it is entirely piss . . . permissible to use it as a bloody metrical device all you bloody want, as you have been bloody doing in conser . . . conversation, anyway, for a century. Just too bad Banjo Paterson could not avail himself of it. Woulda trebled his output."

"Here, don't be knocking the culture. Bloody islanders, I dunno!"

"Culture! Your lot still bans *Lady Chatterley*, Playboy, and the *Ulysses* movie. Shite. I am too crook tonight, eh, to give you the level of insults you deserve, as an unelected representative of this bloody country."

"Har bloody har. Gonna go on again about charter flights from Sydney to New bloody Zealand to see that *Ulysses*? Odd dates for men, and even for women, reckon I have heard it all. Apex of culture you lot have over there. Look: what the hell is that?"

A full moon was rising opposite the last glimmer of the sun's afterglow. Huge, yellow, demonic. And the whole countryside watched and listened. The trace of breeze froze, a faint chorus of ghostly birds murmured across the mulga, only to hush as the moon disc sliced and restitched and blanched to silver as it climbed out of the eastern fug. Then the flies came back, as for a new dawn, and crawled upon their skin, across their shoulders and ear lobes and lips and eyelids. Bruce turned up the lamp to try to distract them, but the flies needed no more light. He turned it off when a clatter of beetles on the glass added another irritant. Both sat on the edges of folding chairs, weakly lashing damp rags over shoulders and wiping faces. The earth radiated its heat back at the moon sullenly.

"Jesus wept, it's still 107 degrees," said Willy.

"Don't believe that thingy. It got fried in the glove box; it has a bubble. Shite. I think I have a bubble. See if there's any ice left in the thinger."

"Already looked. SOL, mate."

"I want my mama. Or yours, in a pinch. What's her name again?"

"Har bloody har."

So bright, sharp-edged shadows demarking black and silver ground, celestial and hadean space. Bruce went on with the crossword in the moonlight.

"Hey, give me one of your long words for *shrewdness*, ten, eleven, twelve letters, or so."

"Hell. Look at yourself. No fucking pants and a crossword a hundred miles from the nearest woman and a hundred degrees warmer than a decent beer. Got serious doubts about you Bruce."

"Glad they sent you to keep me on the level, mate."

"*Perspicacity*. To tell the truth I am a bit bloody crook."

"Perspicacity! Eureka, you are good for something after all!"

"Yeah, well that came from somewhere other than my cranium. Might try to write some notes in the log, though the mind . . . is not so bright as that bugger out there."

So Willy wrote:

The Ballad of P Mack

> Way back then
> All a these jokers was roamin' in the bush
> Goin' where their wheelbarrows led 'em to push
> With hammer, pick, and shovel, and a swag in a pile
> And a bloody wooden wheel remembering every bloody mile
> Bloody queer men.
>
> Way out of Menzies there's a bit of granite rise
> And a run of bloody mulga in a plague of bloody flies
> Meets a salt lake flanked with gypsum bloody dunes
> A soak hole on the rise is oasis to the roos
> A score of black goannas race to dive into the ooze:
> *Dead Mans Soak.*

There's a biscuit tin lid nailed on a stake
And a script punched in it with a nail:
    P Bloody Mack
    Killed by bloody blacks
    Thirty bloody one years old

Forget the bloody date
1894 about
And that was all she bloody well told.

Right about then
Paddy bloody Hannan had a bit of a smile
Up to his armpits in the Golden Mile
'Gold's here, men!'

Bankers said thanks.

And they named the main street after that Paddy Hannan,
You can get fresh water there at the bloody fountain
That is the bloody water bag of Paddy done in bronze:
They pipe the bloody stuff 300 miles from the coast.

You could walk upon the water
But you wouldn't think you oughter
Out at P bloody Mack's
Bloody bloody bloody queer men

After that, he rolled out his cot and tried to lie on it. A nausea came over him, and he sat up quickly and threw up a turbulence of peaches. More water then, he thought, but could not bring himself to get up for the canvas water bag hanging on a branch, until he exhorted himself, bloody bloody bloody.

"Whatsup, mate?" from Bruce, who was shambling around, naked but for his boots and undies, swishing at himself with the crossword, pen behind the ear leaking an inky stain down his stubble. "It's a bit much, innit? Wotcher been writing? Kiniva look? Cor, it's personal. I thought it was geosophy."

"You can read it if you want. It might be my last . . . last will and testament by tomorrow."

"Umm, bit of poetic license there. It ain't a biscuit tin lid, and you do know the date—it's right there on the opposite page. Have to see how it sounds in the daylight, eh? Course, you really look like you might be a corpse in the daylight. You better push that water."

"How you your . . . yourself, mate. You're red and slurred . . . blurred."

"I'm shagged bloody knackered, mate. Lemme stick that thermometer under your tongue after I pull it outa me arse. Hold this wet cloth under your armpit. 'N tie this rag, see, under the chin. Righto. Let's see here. A hungred and three! That's about the same in as out! Two more degrees gets you a free ride on any passing helicopter!

"Sit up. Gonna run the water bag over your head and shoulders. Better move that log book. It's gonna be material evidence, yeah? See if you can take your own pulse, mate. Didya multiply by five or six? Okay, that's human, anyhows."

***

"Get up, mate. I'm taking you in. We're all packed."

What a what? Packed?

"Daylight in a bit. Fewer stakes on this fence line, I hope. Couple hours, depending, to Kalgoorlie, or at least a windmill with a trough to roll you in. Drink that bloody water. Be all the nurses you can eat in a jiffy . . . "

Bruce arranged Willy in the back of the Land Rover, with stuff piled either side. He drove with intense concentration and only had to change one flat, hung unrepaired, on the tail gate. Fingers crossed. When he got to a track away from the fence, he picked up speed a little, and suddenly—*sproing*! through a three-wire, newer fence.

Curses. He stopped to write down the mileage. Thought, *will call the station later.* Then, as the trail improved and his forehead unknit, he replayed, in a corner of his mind, another frantic trip.

They had come up on a white dust cloud on a main road, bulldust deep and malignant, kicked up by a semi-truck ahead of them. They pulled over to let it get ahead, but resumed when the dust cloud died down. In a mile or so, they came upon the wreck: a VW Beetle trying to pass the truck in the dust wedded head-on with a Holden ute in the subsided dust cloud of car-carrying semi-trailer. The ute driver was stoic and silent. The kid in the Beetle, now origami, had both forearms broken, with splintered bones protruding from each. Bruce dragged out their first aid kit: a mystery suitcase. Always wanted to know what was in there—hoping . . . Hey, codeine, snake bite kit, inflatable splints with zippers—the latter a novelty and marvel to all. Bruce and Willy tested the splints on each another. One arm and one full leg, the latter a bit trickier to apply here, too long for a forearm, but it has to do, eh? Holding the kid's fingertips, Bruce wrapped the splints on and zipped them, while Willy held the arms to keep the bones from slipping back under the skin, the ashen kid watching bemused. The truck driver had unloaded a number of cars to get a station wagon down. The ute driver put a jerry can of fuel in its tank, and the kid was laid in the back on Willy and Bruce's cot pads, propped on either side by boxes and with feet elevated. Willy towed the wreckage of Beetle and ute off the road with the Land Rover. The truck driver in the station wagon headed out for Carnarvon, eighty miles away, with Bruce leaning over the laid-back seat to monitor the kid, and Willy drove the Rover, with the silent ute driver, fading and holding his side in the passenger seat, as comfortable as a rabbit in a trap it began to seem. As the station wagon set out, Willy had said to the kid, "Hey, kid, don't worry. Pretty soon'll be all the nurses you can eat." A silent laugh from the ute driver, head tipping back with closed eyes, wrinkles deepening.

***

A nurse said, "Wow, pretty cool splints. Never seen the like, eh," and Bruce said, "That'll be our Canadians, eh?"

"Well I'd say they might even have saved his life, he's going to be OK."

Willy said, "Ute driver never even told me his name. Several broken ribs they say. Spartan bugger."

***

  # Perth

Willy opens his eyes, sees rotund bloke with clipboard. Hmm, he thinks, should get one of them myself in self-defense. Close eyes now and shut the bugger out till, what, till I get a grip? Memory empty, but sloshing. Holy shit. Let it fill up with curses. Unsteady ground. Is there no solid ground? There are white, or maybe green, walls, feet (mine?) sticking up under white cover. He sees me looking – bugger.

"Wha-where am I?" he ventures.

Yeah, you tell me.

"Well, where do you think you are?" asks the tubby cove with a cheerful corpse look.

"Something like p-purgatory, is it?"

"Well, ain't you sparky for a heatstroke near-fatality," says clipboard. "I'm going to propose you are ready for some cognitive testing, check your wiring over. You've been out for a couple of days, but now it might be almost time to send you back out, to chase the mother lode as they say." Watching for reaction, pen poised, then rushing.

Willy looks out the high, narrow window at blue sky, and cringes. Scratch scratch goes the pen.

"Just kidding," says the clipboard. "See a bit of anxiety there about the great outdoors?" And, "We have already done a bunch of tests, but there will be a bunch more before that mental faculty stuff, really. You were pretty comatose there for a bit, kid."

Here comes, what's-her-name, gal from the office, the office, aah. Flowers and everything. And . . . somebody else. Squeak squeak crepe soles.

"Flowers," he says. "What are they called?"

Play it, he thinks, let them tell me. Because . . . bugger it . . . I just . . . don't know. What happened to, ah, that *memory* thing?

Clipboard says, "He recognizes you, anyway, but he has lost a lot. You might have to coach him."

"Katie," he says. That is not it, of course, but . . . "Katie, Katie, give me your answer do," he sings softly in no key. "I'm half crazy . . ."

She blushes. "Fuschias."

"Fuschias? So how are things at the office?"

"We're all worried about you. Several want to come see you. I am the advance scout. How in heck are you doing?"

She has stepped close to squeeze his hand. Yes, she is the draftsperson. From the office that is like a checkpoint you pass through getting an assignment, that answers the phone, that is barely amused at his memo reports; half of them Canadians, not half amused by his anarchist ways.

"Fuschias. I have a bit of um amnesia." Then, slyly, "Hey, did we ever sleep together?"

Mouth drops, then clenches.

"Aha. I see we're going to milk this for every joke and *etcetera*. You know perfickly well, I am a perflickly respickable married woman, you young bugger." Laughs. Has kids. Big-arsed box of Letraset stencils, inky fingers, kinda nice tush leaning over that table. Lois—no; stick with Katie till it comes.

"But Katie, howabout that *etcetera*? I remember . . . "

"You remember what you think you need to. Just don't ask me to go there, you bugger—over the rainbow."

Somebody else, "Bruce will come on in this afternoon. Hopes he can help you through this. He was mighty concerned. He saved you, really." Ah, one of the Canadians, senior, grave humorless grey eyes, not blinking enough for a regular person. Um. Gray? Names a struggle. Rescuing Katie from impropriety he probably thinks.

To the clipboard guy Willy says, "I would like a clipboard and stuff. Maybe with my name on it."

Closes eyes; rude, yes; but then he is very suddenly out of it.

***

Here's Bruce. With a gal. Willy tries not to stare at her, glossy smile, very . . . what? Looking coyly at him, as if maybe she knows him.

"Bruce," he says. "And who's this?"

"Yeah, mate, this one is a bit of a stretch. Three Rivers station?"

Pieces coming at him like big rain drops on the leading edge of cloudburst. He sees a camp on the edge of a yellow dolomite ridge, traces of malachite up and down, the big rain, stuck for a week. Station owner and wife sun-dried, tough, handsome actually, she a tawny raisin in the sun, glistening grape in the verandah shade, with always a chorus and shimmer of hundreds of cockatoos, tame as lambs. Two daughters home for holidays, drove out to camp, straight from the woolshed and sheep dagging, asexual and relishing the stench of being station hands, curious about the geologists camped near the abo sacred spot ("Don't drive there, eh?") and prospecting, whatever that meant. Their sacred spot, too—the backside of the impossible homestead they would always be from but could not live on.

Holy shit, this is one of them. Willy gets a bit emotional, and actually his eyes water up. He whispers, "Holy shit."

"C'mon, I'm not that bad," she says, and is clearly touched that he is dumbstruck at her transformation, though uncertain he really recognizes her, given Bruce's caution when imploring her to visit with him.

"Cind . . . Cinderella," he says. "Bruce, where did you find this one, you bugger?"

"Called her mum. Tracked her down," says Bruce. "Cute, ain't she?"

"Jays love, your mum gave that one your number?"

"Aw, he cleans up alright too, eh? Anyways, he sort of rescued you, eh?"

Bruce shuffles his feet, gripping the back of the visitor's chair. "Course, I wasn't sure I was going to get him outa that trough. Bloody near drowned him," he says under his arm to the girl.

"I don't remember all of that," said Willy. And to her he says, "Did he call you out of the blue and craftily beg you to come . . . come, ah, succor the patient, or are you an item?"

Har humph and a bit of hand wringing from each. Yes, it is a developing thing here.

"I would advise you to snag a lawyer," said Willy. "This guy is not a real blond, and he cannot cook canned peaches for shit.

"And sister?" asks Willy. Neither name is actually coming to mind.

"She couldn't come today," says this one. MacAllen, that's it. He remembers a blackfeller who had been bitten on the toe by a snake. The blackfeller could not say what kind in English, but agreed with whatever Mrs. Mac suggested. Small, yars, or bigger, yars, and she struggling with a razor with the foot hard as a root, then giving up, telling him to go rest up in the shearers' quarters. Makes him queasy again now. He sees himself being queasy, and *hears a clinical voice uttering some drivel somewhere he cannot place. Ow, here it comes again. Language falls away, the girl is speaking, he hears and does not, eyes slide, looking for, what, then stare. Stare. For thirty seconds he loses verbal awareness with eyes wide open.*

Drifting back, he finds Bruce and the girl have gripped his wrists, the girl is feeling for his pulse and ringing the buzzer.

"Ah, had another spell, have we?" says nurse, entering. Sweeping, taking charge, "young bugger" sort of glance.

"Pulse regular, about fifty," says the girl.

Willy hears that these are words he knows but does not comprehend what they are about or mean, for a bit.

"Spell," he says. "Shit."

Bush talk comes back first, then slowly he rises, like a swimmer in a billabong to the blue sky, and breathes phrases back into the lungs. He looks at the nurse, purses a trial "Ooooo," then says, "Tell them." Tell them, let me listen, just be here, here be listening, tell, gawn.

"N-nurse," he cajoles.

"So, he had some brain trauma, bit of kidney shock, too, though that is pretty much over. Result is these fuzzy bits we call 'awareness seizures' or 'absences', sort of like a kind of epilepsy. We have him on a new drug, supposed to knock that right on the head. As it were. We need to observe him for a while, of course."

"Crikey." "Bugger." "Epilepsy!"

"Yeah, crikey is right," says Willy, rising to the female presence, but slurring it around the thermometer. "Could be contagious too, eh?"

Nurse says, "Epilepsy is just a name for a number of neurological things, it does not mean a lot, but the new drugs seem to work across a lot of the spectrum. As for being contagious, it is about as infectious as his sex appeal." Concluding with a sharp tap on his foot-of-bed chart.

Smiles. Supposed to kick his humor, lift the spirits, Willy knows, but he sags. The mind skates on the surface of wit over muddy depths where all the other stuff is. Settling perhaps; pieces come back, much subsides into dark; where it should be, right? But I am, well, slow.

"It is not just the spell, the fainting," he perhaps says, "but the rest that leaks away." Did I say that? he thinks. Or did it cross the mind and not the vocal chords? He cannot tell. And then he cannot recall what he was just thinking. Oh, tired again, still tired.

Bruce says, "Striated. Do you remember that?"

"Striated due to . . ."

"*Striated due to the oscillatory combination of cube and pyritohedron.*"

"Yes, shit. I mean, tell it again."

"Dana on pyrite," Bruce tells the gal. "Willy actually reads his old mineralogy book in the passenger seat, trots out phrases like that about pyrite, used to say those Keats and Yeats chappies could never have done that—'striated due to the oscillatory combination of cube and pyritohedron.' Went into a bar cackling that one and the place was dangerously silent for a minute."

"Whoo. Where *was* that, Bruce?"

"Aw, one of those awful places near Meekatharra, Sandstone maybe, with the pasteurized beer and rabid dog inclined to take offense on behalf of your romantic poets. Hole in the wall for abos to get beer without coming in."

"Poets. I had a black dog for a while." Sorry, all circuits are currently busy with static. Eyes see, why no tell? Black dog: Barney that was, I think, some . . . person's, bit kid on bike in the 'burbs, going to be put down, took him with me a couple of months, became my shadow, then relinquished to a new home, cannot recall how. Hope it worked out for you, old bud, *got your mind right.*

The girl is fondling some object in her pocket. Car keys? No. "Hey, Bruce. You give her that tektite?" Where in hell did that come from he thinks.

She laughs awkwardly and shows it: knuckle-sized heavy black meteorite impact stone, odd aerodynamic shape, its desert rime polished first in Willy's pocket after he and Bruce practically banged heads bending to pick it up from quartz and laterite float, until it wore or found a hole and escaped. Recovered from the Land Rover floor by Lasse, who gave it to Bruce when he left to return to Sweden. Handed-about messenger from over the rainbow, chilled spark of beyond.

"Me mum has a few of these," she murmurs.

"Ah, but not one shaped like that, a cockatoo's dumbbell, a wobbler, I reckon."

Willy stares, picturing the flocks of screeching birds. She and Bruce see his mind going off into the trees, are startled by the shrewd guess and then his drifting away.

They are leaving, Bruce and . . . the Mac. Because his eyelids closed for three breaths. Backing up with mumbles to the nurse.

"Hey Mac," he manages. "Come back, bring Sis."

She stops, hand over mouth to cover uncertainty, joke check.

"Mac!" exclaims Bruce. "I did tell her about P bloody Mack." Waiting to see if he has been dismissed or recalled.

"You go on. Irish is gonna take care of me. Get my mind right."

Bruce guffaws, swipes the side of his nose, and leads the Mac out. Look at them gams.

"Nice cuppa tea," Nurse says. "You are coming around quicker. Going to be another couple of blokes in this room tomorrow, but you . . . I think I'm going to kick you out to the regular ward, or send you home, so you don't have a chance to cause trouble with them."

Home? Couple guys?

"Well, what was all that about back there?" asks nurse. "Who is Irish, for one?"

"Oh, it's you are my Irish. You are the nurse. If you were a pom, you would be the clipboard guy. And then I could not love you."

"Oh, you really take—"

"And Mac is from a station we worked on up north. And getting my mind right: Bruce and I drove a hundred miles on bush trails out of the Woodline Hills to get to N-Norseman a couple years ago, to see *Cool Hand Luke* at the drive-in. Did ya see it? No? Paul, yes, Paul

Newman is the dude. The warder guys tell him he has to *get his mind right*. But guess what."

"Irish, I don't have a home," he went on. "I live out of a company Land Rover, and when I'm in town I stay in a hotel. And now I cannot even drive for a bit."

"Are you . . . ? Jesus wept. And I'm not Irish." She is unsettled by his scrambled rush of memory and rude jollity.

"Shall I tell you about P Mack?"

"Why don't you save it for later, sweetie? I have more 'n just you to take care of."

"Ah, 'sweetie' it is now? L-lollies in a bag, one after another."

She is a bit grim now, busybodies about and gone. No ring, thirties, feet getting flat. Be nice with those footsies in the air though, eh?

His mind is foggy with waves of gloom. Bar somewhere near Meekatharra: he cannot recall any of this but for a flash on the two foot square window in the back wall, through which the aboriginals were served beer. Ouch. How could that be? Sees himself standing there, perplexed, partly in horror that he is standing there perplexed. Which calls up another spot of horror. As a child he was obliged to dig a hole in which three kittens with ringworm were placed then shot with shotgun, after which he'd had to fill in the hole. What was his father thinking, to enroll him in that? What crater in his psyche did that hide in, and how is it called up with the awful bar, as fleeting poltergeists in the darker vapors of this damaged mind? All of the guilt of his own shortcomings, and the shit in which he is only a swimmer, can, it seems, be thrown at him at any time by this randomly resurgent, broken memory machine. Bloody bloody hell.

P bloody Mack; okay. I wrote it like Banjo Paterson, a doggerel yarn. Bruce thinks the blacks are just another megafauna heading for extinction, after themselves extinguishing a whole lot of Pleistocene megafauna like the bunyip. Of course, the sheep stations will not last either. The MacAllens will get pushed into the "Palladial Fringe" rest homes by nylon and rayon. Maybe two, three thousand generations of blacks here since they crossed over from Asia, and the Macs will not make four up there. Grandfather Mac drove merinos three hundred miles overland from Carnarvon; must have followed the rivers, digging in sand beds to find them water. Nation builders and natives walking dream-lines colliding at water holes. As told by the pen and punch of the whites. Us.

Yes. Driven men who staked out an existence in an empty end of the world, and therein their dynasties. All quite humble supermen. More than a few station homesteads occupied by son and daughter heirs in clandestine double shade: my sister (my wife). Each ignoring, but in time discovering elements of the substrate, the walkabout tracks of three thousand generations of blackfellers, some representatives of whom stopped to trade some time for baccy money. The Macs, a self-forged aristocracy of the terrain formerly unoccupied by Europeans, but not quite empty. P Mack's assailants.

Bit odd, eh, the blackfellers did not experiment in those thousands of generations with iron in the Hamersleys. Thousands of square miles of iron oxides, with fulgurites all over the place; fulgurites, lightning-struck hollow tree trunks that is, filled with sand by ants and vitrified, iron on silica glass. Don't reckon Hephaestus gave that kind of hint to those Mediterranean rascals. But . . . Abos and Kalahari bushmen on their laterites. How often did they see and decline the murderous iron, decline to enslave iron in forge?

Bit of a funk here, Willy-me. Black bloody gloom running away with me. Try ringing the bell perhaps. Even a cross word, please, Nursey. But no. She said she is busy, and would ignore me if not. Pissed her off, in fact. Dearest nurse, tell me your secret name. Secret name! That is something Lasse said. What she'll say, *Enema time for you, boy-oh*. Gotta write to that Lasse in Sweden.

Think about something else. Bruce and that gal, imagine them dagging sheep. Had to tell Bruce one day that a dag had some different connotations in New Zealand, not just clattering balls of dried shit on the hindquarters of sheep (hence "rattle your dags"), but also the "bit of a dag," meaning a comic, a wag. "C'mon. Youse guys are supposed to be the Cockney rhyming heirs," he had said, leading inevitably to allusions to sheep-shaggers, and to "Shit, it's your lot has that fixation and this, shall we say, sensitivity to being called a dag. If *sensitivity* can be used in regard to your tribe." All in good humor, though it was understood should a jolt from a pothole in the road break the banter before reaching a wisecrack resolution, the brutal heat could char it to grit between the teeth, needing a beer rinse soon as possible. It is not easy being almost handcuffed to one person in that damn country.

Now it seems unlikely I can go back out there, at least for a while. How do I feel about that? Maybe I should feel rescued. I was going crazy out there, tropo, and is this my wages?

***

Dear Lasse

Hope you are well and have caught up on your female quota since getting home to Sweden from the Great Orange Corroboree. The crows miss you, they are always complaining, awrk.
I had a bit of a turn. Got heatstroke somewhere out there and suffered a bit of neural damage. I am recovering but cannot drive until it is clear these drugs have stopped the lapses of consciousness, and am struggling to regain memory, which has random holes, some big and others bigger. Bruce brought in one of those MacAllen girls from Three Rivers station, the ones that came to the camp like gypsies off a road crew, and she was pretty cute all scrubbed up like a model, and I still cannot recall her name, damn it.

So I am a bit useless at present and not ready to venture back into the bush, have a dread of the heat as well as doctor's 'No don't go'. I have a wild notion to come visit you, try the northern summer, sit in a small boat on a lake, check out your old school and that geophysics department, and recuperate and do something completely different all at the same time. Restore or scrape and build new, whichever comes first.

I know you must be busy with some sort of life and I do not expect to be your guest, just let me hear from you the slightest lack of discouragement and watch out. With the help of Nurse I have applied for a passport.

Best etc, Willy Mills

***

Bruce tracked Willy down in a boarding house in Subiaco once he was discharged, on rest and daily checkups.

"Brucellosis! Welcome to the tiny streets of Subiaco. Home of, um, the working Eyetie class of Perth."

"Gidday, Willy. Took a while to find this possie, eh?"

"Yeah, it's far out, or in. This is by the week, kinda quiet, though no really good place to read out of earshot of the telly, but, you know, just patiently waiting. I can walk to the library to read as much as the head will let me, anyhow. And, hey, they have several actual books over there, maybe even twelve."

"Uh huh."

"What's up, Bruce? You look as if somebody died."

"Yeah well."

"Oh shit."

"Trish MacAllen."

"That Three Rivers? Oh shit. Crikey Moses!"

"Yeah. You mighta heard about it. They didn't release the name until today. Parachuting."
"No, bugger me, that was Miss Mac? The younger?"

"Yup." Longish silence. "They say she seemed level enough, went through Wednesday orientation class enthusiastically, jumped on the Saturday, in harness, off the roof, with a whoop, and on the Sunday they were dropped offshore, supposed to sail inland on the sea breeze looking at the schools of sharks before touching down atop the cliffs. The main chute didn't open like it was supposed to on the automatic cord thing, and she didn't pull the backup chute cord."

"Unnnhhh!"

"Mandy says she was depressed about the prospect of living forever in the city, giving up on the station, which only works, the station that is, if you find a husband at Roxby Downs week. You know—the bush horse race thing. But that wouldn't explain the main chute failure. So. Dunno?"

"Uhhh. Jeez, Bruce, I'm sorry. How is your Mac with it?"

"Mandy? I haven't seen her. Cremated Sis quietly, ceremony's gonna be up at the station. Damn."

A shuffling silence.

"Hey Bruce, I would drive up with you to that funeral if . . . "

"Jeez Willie, I would go eh? I wasn't invited. I think it is a family affair. One minute everyone is going in a radius of two, five hundred miles, then it is, well, as if it was a suicide."

"Bruce, mate, you're a bit keen on that gal?"

"Ah well, Willy, I sorta was, then I was shut down. Kinda made to feel not really a member."

"Aw shit, Bruce, I'm sorry. I suppose I should write them a something. Did you send a card?"

"Yeah, one or two."

"Think you oughta go up there, Bruce. Show 'em a photo of your testicles, tell 'em they need your genes, and you can learn to dag sheep with the best of them. I mean, a mother-in-law that trails clouds of parakeets and cockatoos of every known species like the Queen of the Night, all screaming her name."

"Willy, your gonads are showing, eh? Besides, that's the river that brings the galahs in, not Her Highness. But you know, Willy, your pontificating is coming back. Reckon that's a good sign, eh? Hey, what's this? You're reading that Voss again, or still?"

"Again, mate. Having a hard time reading, actually, holding a thread. Bit like trying to stand up inside an old hedge."

"You said once or maybe a couple of times you were, what, unenthusiastic about similes. Maybe you oughta stay away from them a bit longer, till you get 'em under control. Hey," he goes on, " I see you've drawn that P Mack's plaque inside the cover. That's cool. Not getting a bit maudlin about it, are we?"

"Ah hell mate, I don't know."

"You know, if you were sticking around, I would say, get another dog, someone to talk to. But hey, what did the company say to you?"

"Severance, mate. Generous. Surprised you didn't hear their sigh of relief that I said *just fine*. I cannot go bush for a while and would be bugger all use in the office. Can't hardly stand it. And I'm ready for the Big Escape."

"Yeah? Like how?"

"I'm going to see Lasse, see about a mellow summer and maybe grad school up in that Sweden."

"No. Really? Hey, almost forgot, I brought you something."

Bruce takes a folded piece of paper out of his pocket. "Sally dug this up for you in the downtown library. She copied it out of some archive by hand. I'll read it to you since your eyes look a bit strained, but I'll leave it with you.

"Cor bloody Sweden!"

Sally! Aha, that's her name, Katie the drafter gal. What then? "Whatsit Bruce?"

"It's that P Mack. I told her about it and she was intrigued. There's a reference on the bottom, but this is the guts of what it said about Mack:

"Mack was a prospector and trail blazer, who was attacked by natives on 14 July 1894, and died 3 days later. Phil Mack and his mate Sunshine Fowler from western New South Wales came to the west to find gold ... They pulled up to camp at the rocks where Mack met his death. It is said he was kneeling making a damper, with seemingly friendly natives looking on, but they were Wall-eye Joe, famed for his cunning and his two gins. One of the women engaged Mack's attention drawing lines on the ground to indicate the whereabouts of water. The man had found their small axe used to cut tent pegs and dragging it along with his toes, struck Mack over the head. Sunshine rushed to his assistance and received a blow on his hand nearly severing his fingers. There was another party of men camped nearby and shouts quickly brought assistance, but it was too late for poor Mack."

"Ha! Dear Sally! Fancy that! God Bruce, an epi-, whatsit, epitaph for a fellow lunatic! I oughta go over to that downtown library tomorrow myself! Look Bruce, give Sally a big kiss for me, I'll bring her some flowers.

"Bruce mate. Look, even if I am not dead in the bush I am anyway fucked here. I am not sure who I am. Cannot even drive. Hang onto my hammer and compass in case I come back, but I have to find, well, god knows what. Whether it is the old arsehole or something new, I do not know. Uhnn. Look, I'll swing by that office soon. Ain't going to be anything drawn out, but I'll probably see you then, I reckon."

But quite possibly not, they both think. No drawn-out goodbyes between bush mates.

***

Willy goes to see the neurologist. He feels oddly as if he is struggling to escape the *naked-and-homework-not-done dream,* up to see the headmaster. Although he assured the nurse he could find the neurologist's office down the street, he insisted she draw him a map with the address on it, *just in case*, but then she went off to her post to put it together, no volunteering to escort him with her somehow-steadying antiseptic aura. Guess that is what *out-patient* means.

"When was the last one?" asks neurologist.

"While I was still in that hospital, I think two weeks ago?"

"That's good. Howsabout those peripheral visions, voices, sort of thing?"

"Sometimes a . . . a thinning of presence and feelings of gaps, and expectation of . . . of that damn droning voice at the right shoulder, but I cannot explain it to myself at the time, and then after I cannot recall it in words to tell it."

An encouraging silence. Listening, I guess he would say. Does not blink. Probably has done seminar on controlling your professional demeanor. But OK.

"So, Doc, I scribbles in my notebook but it's empty chatter. And the memory—I don't remember what I've forgotten, but it's like plutons subsided and some erupting again, tangled, not called for, and some lost. I cannot remember names, is one thing else. And I am slow. I often don't get the punchline until sundown."

"How are the spirits otherwise?"

"Do you mean the sarcasm or . . .? I sometimes stare, then say something off the wall. You can see them think, Is this guy tropo?"

"I mean, from our earlier conversations you let on you were a bit depressed before the stroke, and I recommended you see a therapist."

"Yis. I have not. Afraid to lose my footing between the fuzzy bits."

"I told you we can find you a therapist who understands the neural, neurological damage and would not torture you for things you have just forgotten. Or what you think is banal. Look, it's clear your absences were caused by stroke damage and are being, seem to be, controlled by the drug, but it is common for such things to lead to morbidity, even if you were ah, a socialite before. For which, I mean morbidity now, there are also some helpful drugs. By the way, I'm recommending upping the dose of the Clorazepate about a half, to keep the voice and other peripheral stuff at bay. I could also prescribe an antidepressant."

"Maybe in a week, the shrink. *Stuff,* you say. A useful medical term, I suppose."

"Yes, stuff, but never nonsense, professionally. Good-oh on the therapist, but call now and make an appointment, eh?"

***

Willy at the shrink: he does not understand what this person wants, his questions are out of some antique text book, falling like very large rain drops on his face, ominous, *wind dust and hail to follow*. *How do I feel about my father*? What? Wallpaper shows vinyl disregard for gastric equilibrium. Willy looks for possible shelter under large potted plant leaves. He takes a breath and blurts to, ah, distract from that *still-missing homework* feeling.

It is a blank, truly an absence, I know, not an enlightenment. You assure it is meaningless and less interesting than the stuff in the crazy-bugger manual; you mock my looking for the meaning. Yes, damn, all right, I do it to myself. That blankness descending, yeah, it's not superintelligence, it's subintelligence. Perhaps it's what you feel with a spear in your side as you ebb from the world. It's dumb, vivid, livid, not metaphorical. Yeah, now I'm horny and depressed again, or still. Gotta face that music, we reckon, but, hey, I have this un-thing that happens. It is somewhat incapacitating—cannot drive, hardly read more than snatches, you know, I lose the thread. I cannot . . . Your silence, you think to provoke anger, release. That is therapy: unravelling; but I am not as it were ravelled. I am visited by the absence thing, no, I do not, like, *possess* it, I can't even recall it, except it is a reset, and I remember it happens. I do not say *guiding light*, but, okay, it doesn't really matter, I think we're done here. Going out that door, little bit of paranoia door might be locked, side effects of Dopadummie or a century of Freudian license. Hah. No, that was not liberating, it was, what. Already to be forgotten!

***

Chapter 3

Voyage to Older Worlds

Willy gave away most of what he owned, except quite a bit of money saved by living austerely, mailed a tea chest of books to himself in that Uppsala, Sweden, got a godawful short-cropped haircut at a maleficent barber, and got on a plane.

Crossing Australia in daylight, south to north, he saw no familiar landmarks—not a butte, not a scar where anyone had dug a Land Rover out of a playa, and certainly not the hollow and soak where rest the remains of P. Mack. Yet, so much orange with unbelievably tenacious green speckle. He did not have a window seat but gazed, sometimes, through the door porthole. A school mate had related how they tried flashing mirrors at high flying planes when their Land Cruiser cratered and they walked across a quad map to a soak, and ate a couple of kangaroos cornered in an arc of mulga brush and killed with geology hammers for two weeks until their boss happened on them in a Cessna on Christmas Day. He tried to recite to himself the ballad of P. bloody Mack, at sundown, at the porthole in the exit door, lost the thread, went back to his seat, and slept on to Singapore, where it was raining in the dark, raining from sky and ground and every pore of every human in the airport, in which they were allowed an hour to get from one gate to another.

A dozen Nepal-bound hipsters on the last flight were not on the next plane.

His new plane was an Air India 707, starting out half full and picking up lots more people in places where continuing passengers were not allowed off—Madras, perhaps? He was too groggy to take stock when arriving full in Bombay in the dead of night. Which was apparently not yet equipped to deal with jumbos, one of which they were supposed to transfer to, so they were herded down rolling stairways and bussed across tarmacs to a hangar. A bit claustrophobic in such dense crowds of people, many of whom exuded unfamiliar odors of oils and perfumes and tobaccos. He lagged in the rear as the plane's disgorged human cargo stumbled into the hangar. A contingent of khaki-clad and turbaned Sikhs encircled the crowd and ushered it into one corner: not a chair, or a sign to be seen, just a vast concrete floor up to arched steel shadows.

As anxious passengers milled, and some waved their passports and tickets, the Sikhs shrugged and strolled the perimeter. He found himself against a wall with a lean, tired, perhaps Dutch-speaking woman with three kids (bump nose declining to entertain hint of any smile it was designed for) all moaning on the grumpy edge of sleep. She sat against the wall, breast-feeding the baby, a toddler and a six-year-old clutching a small camera crumpled across her legs.

An hour passed. Then another crowd was ushered into the other end of the hangar, and re-enacted the scene a hundred yards off in the dark; another 707's complement, voices of indignation and protest, a far murmur that dampened the complaint in his corner.

A set of doors suddenly lit and opened in the middle of the hangar, beyond which was a set of gates for screening tickets, and Willy's lot was roused and escorted in a quick trot toward them. The Dutch woman stirred and clutched her children. Loud noise; and the second 707 crowd crushed in behind them. The Sikhs had been replaced by a new beardless shift in greener uniforms, who penetrated the roiling cacophony to enforce lines, shouting back at cranky passengers in pungently various alphabets. Now he and the woman were side by side, she uttering occasional words to the clinging children, one sagging and pulling on her dress, and in the crush, he picked the one off the floor from underfoot, which immediately squirmed onto his shoulder and zonked as he and the mum exchanged soft glottals sounding like what-the-hell-sort-of-baby-thief-is-this and just-helping-through-this-crowd, and he stuck close behind her, sidling as the agents puzzled over their being, or not being, together, barking at their own confusion and at the two whites, until bang, thump, stamps and shouts and hurry-ups, emerging under night sky, still the crowd which thrust and pulsed on all sides, we are getting onto buses, and, hello, where did she go? Wait. Willy did not even know her name to shout. Surely she will scream. Green uniforms parted the crowd: you lot go on, the rest wait; he looked for a hand to go up as the greens pushed with batons. Oh shite, so loud. He pushed to the front, was pushed back into the throng on the steps as the buses pulled out. A fellow next to him shouted at a green and pointed at him. The green glared.

Commotion; and a bus stopped, greens flurried as the bus door opened, and here came Mama, storming with arms full. Unconscious child number two was yanked from him and he was pulled out the edge of the crowd. The oldest child had stepped down from the bus, too, and snapped a camera at him. Oh bugger me! Suddenly, he was a kidnapper! Mama halfway back to the bus, carrying two and trailing one child on her skirts, turned and screamed a burst at the greens detaining him.

"I was just holding it," Willy said to the space where he expected the arresting officer would appear. All of the greens in earshot froze, confused. She got on the bus, he stepped back, the fellow behind tapped his elbow and asked, "Why did you take her child?" "Because she could not carry them all." "There will be *trouble*." Wait, that was the first English he'd heard in a while, but who spoke it? A trilling musical English, making him suddenly cringingly conscious of his own bumpkin accent.

So, poised in humiliation in the dark between one crowd merging with another, under the stares of greens and the restless cargo, he waited for *trouble* in bewilderment. Then another bus pulled in and he was swept in like just another envelope in a mail bag; and off. Pulled from a dubious limelight back into the shadowed stream, he thought, The story is not about us, two white people at the nub of the dark mass. Ah. Wrong script, too bad, no I should be relieved.

A 747 it is: 500 plus passengers. He remembered Barraclough saying, "Never catch me in one of they new 747s. Imagine an hysteria running through them." It was chock full. The mass seethed, burrowing into hard seats, and pillows and things stuffed in then brought back out of overheads and bags, charging sleep-ward, last mutterings in ten languages of disgust at the hangar, as residua of the trouble dissipated. No English in his vicinity in the last murmurs subsiding into ten dialects of breathing. He tried to read, slippery eyes glissading over pages of Patrick White, gaining no hold on ledge or cranny of text; he turned the light out but could not sleep either.

Sometime later he tried to find the young woman. An attendant said there was no other white person on the plane. Ah, on this level, perhaps upstairs? Ah, there is an upstairs; but off-limits to, well, us downstairs. But he wandered as he was able, up the one side and down the other, someplace between stunned and fascinated, eyeing the fellows (and almost all were men); ye gods and us herrings. Peering out at smudges of anonymous cities cast behind in the night, one upon another. Two engines on this wing, what now? Edging back to the other side: three engines on this wing. Underneath him, striding steady air, no rattle of rivets, no, what, currents of passenger unrest? So, off to the purser, a disdainful thin man, born to not work, with a clipboard in a cubby near the galley, dedicated to not appearing to listen.

"Look, no panic, but we have one less engine on the left than on the right. Is that all right? And, ah, can we communicate the issue without causing a panic, sort of?"

Pursed-lip purser, holding back ten languages, faintest curl showing disdain for this accent, again. Aww crikey. Mostly body language said, *Please get out of my way, I have many things to not do.*

On, squashed. Ocean dark, with glimmer of stars fractured by already crazed plane windows; then a swath of flares from the Kuwaiti desert, awful candles of another other world, holy hell. Bedouins drunk on oil with huge fires. Bedouins? Not, of course. Sleep on that for a bit; dreams such as Purgatory was made from, vast noise with only enough self to register insignificance, and uselessness. A child kidnapper with only one language and bumpkin accent merging into the queue for some sorry tomorrow.

Sunrise. And only then the purser was making announcements: wake up for coffee, measured sentences with long pauses, five tongues. "Ladies and gentlemen, it may be noted we have an extra engine on the right side we are transporting to Rome. That is how we do it." Plane dips ever so slightly to one side then the other, but no hysteria, *pace*, Barraclough.

Rome. How to unload a 747. In twenty minutes there was not an Indian to be seen. The plane he left was backed out by tractor and hauled away, so there was no engine removal spectacle for him. In a new concourse he was bemused by a score of male Orthodox Jews bobbing about with phylacteries. This area of the terminal seemed to be out of toilet paper, perhaps that was their problem (*our issue, no tissue! Deliver us from evil!*).

In London all the un-English voices disappeared and a cacophony of potpourri English filled the terminal, as incomprehensible as a dozen black and white British television programs intercut, and he did not understand the questions of the person stamping his passport so he could enter the UK just far enough to go along to another terminal. *Just, passing, through. Bit dazed, sorry. No, don't want visa.*

To Stockholm. Small plane from a far terminal, walking across tarmac and going up rollout stairs, in front of him a seven-foot blonde woman with straight hair to her waist—a troll queen, he presumed—the rest of the passengers men in business suits, all the same grey. Shall I ask them how they see me, he thought. Perhaps I intimidate them, hairy legs poking out of shorts all over pockets . . . Oh, if only he had entertained that thought, and rolled it out with a bloody great Gidday Maties! Too late again, another "shoulda" withered on the vine.

Arlanda. A small airport in the trees on a dark conifer plain. This stands for Stockholm? Stomp stomp, economical courtesies, and onto a curb with a few taxis. Cabbies all, what, middle eastern, anyway, and nary a word of English between them. "Uppsala . . ." Aah, the train, to a station avoiding the city somewhere back there in the woods, then this, then that, like flights of birds harrowing a dusty dusky consciousness, until he reached a spare white room in Hotel Linné , and descended into a mountain of fluff, welling and absorbing the chatter and flavors of half the known world. Down he went, unnumbered duvet fathoms. So that is a duvet, and just the tiniest thought, *Who is this sinking, dear Liza, with what?*

Jolted awake in two seconds from the falling-through-cloud dream. Accustomed to folding cot under the Southern Cross, or orange motel candlewick with the sodium vapor lights outside. Where? Sits up. Hotel Linné; she'll be right. Linnaeus, eh? Jumbled by jet lag, bit like the absences, but we're in the game, yes! Crikey, this is it, just ease onto the side and slide a leg out to warn the scorpions away, and slide back down the edge of that cloud, aah!

***

Willy woke with the light, as always, though the body clock was having conniptions. Outside, a mild leafy sunny day between interfingering town and forest. Twin peaks of a cathedral in one direction, over the trees; walk the path through fields and copses in the opposite direction, yes. Few people. Hungry, me thinks, he thought. So, after a mile or three, he turned around and retraced, toward spires and presumably food. Oops, not the same path, somewhere diverged with eyelids soaking half-closed against the sunrise. Aah.

Coming upon a string of mounds. What? An esker is it? Err, burial mounds? Dolmens on drumlins, looks like. Rail-fenced, with tiny signs, restrained and probably saying, If you climb on the mounds your foreign pecker will be whacked. But no, an older couple with a dog briefly topped one and disappeared again. And soon, coming toward me on the path. I am dressed about as similarly as the loin cloth African meeting Stanley (shorts and sandals), he thought. Say something.

"Good morning."

A sidelong look, disapprobation, not as if threatened by a weirdo but of sages silent in twenty tongues confronted by vagrant. Oh, then he was passed by, and suddenly profoundly lonely. Lonely! Wrong salmon up the creek. Give me a trowel and I will tidy this mound just to be, what, busy. The real self is mislaid in some airplane toilet. Walk purposefully. Where spires gone? Jesus, so far off! Better go back.

Here, town. Wotchercallit, Hanseatic-looking or something, stolidly mercantile, thick walls with small windows and arches, or Puritan, bugger all signs. Where was 'café' or 'meals' or winking neon? Ah, here looked like one, but not open; and another. Nice little river, tumbling into a reach that must have a lock, some small barges even, see, loading grain of some kind, for that Stockholm no doubt. That would be a pretty hitchhike, with parasol and paramour, to sing an aria to along the reedy waters. "If only I could sing," he said aloud. There is a romance to inhabit, if only I were a romantic, but to become something, a lover; give me then a ticklish trollop and champagne for an afternoon on a barge.

Walk-walk-walk. The few people he passed by at this early hour and yes, he counted on fingers, it's Sunday, speaking in alien rhythms: urbanites. Even as his body swung itself along streets and paths and lungs took in northern air and breath by breath shed gaseous vestiges of the south, his head moved above where unfamiliar bird song and faintest ticking of a waking town scarce creased the wooded plain. Invisible, he felt; until there in a shop window he saw his reflection against this scenery and winced: preposterous.

So that was Uppsala north, quite commodius and civilized and refined and sleepy and hungry and not much more than coffee and a *croissant*, with the T emphasized to not be mistaken for French (hah!) pointing at a pastry, maybe tomorrow being Monday he would find something to eat, someone to exchange a few words with. At least cross back over the river and up the hill to that palace or whatever it is next to that cathedral, to scout south woods and whatever. Why are half the cannons on the hill pointing at the cathedral? Sense of humor somewhere in there.

Back inside that duvet at dark in the Hotel Linné, sinking in milky pond with remnant of jet roar transmuting to hush of glacier ghosts grinding on gray and white granite, an esker full of pre-Vikings at rest just up the road.

Journal opened, but no courage to write anything. Buzzz. Salmon up wrong creek I said, or was it wrong salmon in the creek. Think P Mack could have come from this stream? Pick a beck. Have picked. Up the stream of Count Linné, grand classifier, John the Baptist to Darwin, our Prometheus. How did I end up here? Cracked and frayed, through an Air India funnel, now a cork chip afloat in the northern woods. A cool chapel lit by high windows and total peace.

But, he wrote in journal after all, the hermit enters the monastery gate and the first trial is *Loneliness*? Aw, shit on that; loneliness is just laziness, c'mon boys and girls.

***

Chapter 4 Uppsala

A day later he is in new student housing in a development called Flogsta, still under construction, has directions to classes in beginning Swedish, and has a very used and very pink bicycle. The sun, by which he was wont to tell the orientation of the day in time and space, seems a bit confused. Jet lag still; that'll be it. Slight dizziness, eustachians need a drink, he says to hisself.

Lasse appears, his field assistant in West Australia and Tasmania once upon a time. He has just driven, like a rocket it seems, from Umeå. Wherever that is. Some distance off on the Baltic, is it?

"Willy-Willy! I don't believe it! You really are here!" An awkward hug; there's a first.

"Mate, I am sorry I was not here when you came. How do you say? Cousin's wedding in Vaasa, in Finland. Plus hangover!" Willy hears right away the Australian English has already weakened; there is a flicker of struggle in the all-smiles demeanor. "Well, I'll be buggered!" comes through it. Then, "How's the head? I mean, that is to say."

"The head is full of birds and bees and greenery and a bit disoriented yet."

"Do you know anyone here?" Lasse asks in the communal kitchen right off the entrance to Willy's hall.

"A Pole and a Greek who speak no English. Others glimpsed. Some telephoners," indicating communal phone on the wall, "who do not speak English or French or wish to understand mine, anyway. Not amused."

"Well, you need to have a party to meet everyone!"

"Err, right-oh. You can help me find food and liquor stores."

"Hey, howabout peanut butter chicken?"

"Huzza! You know, I did bring the wok in my bag."

"Okay, I do believe it. You are one crazy bugger, Willy. But no Vegemite, no? Let's go. Need marker and paper also, for big notice on door there."

Lasse has little to say about home, family, girl. "You, Willy, should know how it is to go home. Three easy questions you are supposed to answer with 'It was quite interesting, but there's no place like home.' So then man must be serious about reality, job, or else who do you think you are?"

He makes enough chicken and rice for twelve. The Pole Stefan, Rolf the medical student, an Americaner, Jim, and a very young mousy shy gal ("The smoker," he whispers to Lasse) turn up. After a couple bottles of Tinto and a rise in volume, the Greek Andrei and another Swedish gal come in.

"That chicken is fantastic!" says American Jim. Grabs the shoulder of the Elsa; ah, they are together.

"Old and secret Australian family recipe," says Lasse. "Out of some magazine in a toilet, I believe. To be real Australian, the chicken should be stolen."

Getting louder on the fifth bottle of Tinto, more people, including a couple from the neighboring hall. But all stop talking to hear Lasse tell his willy-willy story—Swedish, then a loose English rendition. "Let me tell you how I met Willy.

"Willy was working on his own in the bush. One boss said that was okay, but when the head boss heard, he said that was *not safe*, and all of that. So, the lower boss took me out to work with Willy. He wanted to see what Willy was doing, anyway. He wanted to check some of those maps Willy was turning out. So, we asked a station owner, that is the sheep farmer, where he thought Willy was mapping, if he knows where Willy is, get some general directions, and drive down a dirt road, turn at a gate, and follow fresh tracks down a fence. It is hot and the air is, how do we say, turbulent. We find his camp. Not much, but there are a couple of kitchen boxes and a coffee pot on the grate over a dead fire. We wait an hour, but there is no sign of him. I say, he should be back soon to eat perhaps, there is the coffee pot after all, but the boss wants to go look for him. He has a bad feeling, you can see, he is still feeling, what is it, his own boss's um, unhappiness.

"So, we are driving along a fence very slowly in a cloud of dust, toward a windmill on the map. A windmill, you know, has a well, and usually has a big tank full of water filling a, a trough for sheep. We see the windmill through the trees, low, hard . . . desert trees. Mulga, they call it. Suddenly, here comes Willy running down the fence. He is completely naked, except for sandals on the feet, and he is chasing a willy-willy, which is just here to the side. A willy-willy is a whirlwind, a dust devil, yes? As he gets up to us, we see something—a shirt—in the willy-willy, which moves away into the trees and disappears. Willy comes up to the window and leans on it. 'Well shit,' he says.

"'Willy-willy!' says the boss. And that is about all he can find to say to naked Willy standing with his hand on the Land Rover mirror. The willy-willy has taken his shirt and shorts off a bush while he was in the tank.

"Of course, sandals out there in the bush with all the biting and stinging things and spiny plants and dry sticks and stones gave him a bit of tick- tock pain also. 'This is Lars,' he said."

Lasse mimes as he repeats for Stefan and Andrei, and the others listen for the punch line of the second take. General laughter, building. "Willy-willy!" His name is up there now as if in lights, a test of gossip mechanisms in this part of the world, polyglot shy youths, many newly away from home, briefly unlocked by Tinto.

The smoker's mother turns up in time for the last piece of chicken and a paper cup of Tinto, and, sober, hears recapitulation of some of the buzz from daughter, who is not. Mother seems chuffed that her timid daughter is part of the voluble throng. Mother has brought package with bedding or something, quaffs Tinto, delicately avoids chicken, leaves. Exeunt gradually the others, severally, dribs and drabs, leaving trailing phrases translated by Lasse. The Pole and the Greek have no English and very limited Swedish, are both political refugees and grad students, the one in limnology (It's about lakes! They have lakes here!) and the other in economics for when the junta is overthrown. Rolf, the medical student, is currently learning by rote the names of all two hundred and six bones (or so) in the human body in Swedish, Latin, English, and German, and is at first very light in the handshake, with voice falling and laughter rising through the party, and a little transparent anxiety at retiring that he may have lost a few names. When the smoker goes to her room, Willy asks what her name was, did not catch it, and no-one is quite sure, and Lasse ventures, "Morsdottir, and Dottirsmor, although they might be sisters." Jim and Elsa dispose of paper plates and cups and a dozen bottles. Willy insists on cleaning his wok, nobody else permitted, of course. It excites some curiosity, but too late, boys and girls, it is already tomorrow. Good night to sailors in their ships at sea, to polar bears and bunyips and to me. Lasse will sleep on Willy's floor and leave at daybreak, before five a.m. No, wait, he will take Willy over to the geophysics department first.

Lasse says in the dark, "Stay away from that Morsdottir. Bad for you, Willy. Like you, got the, wotchercallit, melancholy, and, shit, she is only eighteen."

"Oh boy, no sweat."

"Come visit me in Umeå and you can meet some nice Finnish girls who will make you happy to jump into a frozen lake through a hole in the ice!"

***

Lasse takes Willy to a coffee shop and then hauls him over to the university geophysics department. The Prof, head of department, is out, but one who was an undergrad with Lasse is in the basement, now a grad student, so they spend some time waiting for Prof what-the-hell-was-that-name to get out of an admin meeting. Stig here has a mess of lined tractor paper computer printouts and shoeboxes of punch cards, a dozen text books and only feeble apparent life signs. No ho-ho reminiscences. Maybe Lasse pissed in his beer one field project weekend. Stig could have done with some desert time.

The Prof (Willy has no idea what to call him) is immediately affable and likeable and interested to hear about Lasse's time in Australia, where he and his cousins were supposed to try a new array of sensors and some peculiar deconvolutions to take the electromagnetic pulse of the Precambrian bedrock at depth, and, of course, its nickel nodes. Lasse exclaims that Postcambrian scrofula, which is to say the last half billion years, laying on that satanic continent with every permutation of salt and clay minerals made mockery of their methods, and that is why he, Lasse, came to work for Willy's company for a time, to recover some money to get home with. His cousins went to other American companies and have since gone to South America, tangled with nationalizing incivilities, and are not so often heard from. Willy gathers what he never understood before, that the cousins are twins, Americans, but one of them came here to do his thesis.

Lasse skips over a sketch of Willy's heatstroke and says that Willy might like to become a geophysicist in a cooler climate after he has fully recuperated, perhaps Greenland. Probably a wink in there Willy did not catch.

The prof asks Willy what he is doing now, and what his math background is. Willy says he is learning Swedish while he fully recuperates, and his math was never great and is set back a bit. He is working on it.

"Got couple undergrad texts, sometimes okay with complex numbers and sometimes not, have personal hangups with sets gibberish. Sort of fascinated with math as a language here, trying schoolboy French with people in Swedish class and thinking approximations are always interesting, if not trustworthy."

Yes, would have to do some makeup. ODEs, PDEs and matrix algebra, and howabout that physics? Okay; but Willy's spirit is more chilled than thrilled. Damn that Maxwell's electromagnetism, up a flight from my mind capacity now, he thinks.

"Willy is a bit of a poet," says Lasse. "Not what you would think for a geophysics type, but he has some talent as geologist."
"Whoa, Lasse! Poet! That is a harsh thing to say! Like accusing me of religion."

"Nonetheless," offers the prof, beetling from under brows, "geophysics is most often about models, expressed metaphorically in somewhat, well, tedious matrix mathematics. So, send us your transcripts, have a nice fall in Uppsala learning Swedish—good that you are doing that—and come back to see me when you are ready to discuss options. We could possibly start you in one way or another in January, if it all worked out."

"I should say," says Willy, "I know I was just a consumer of the product, but we had great maps of Australia showing airborne aeromagnetics and gamma, flown by the government, which we all used like road maps, showing the old greenstone belts and the granite batholiths in the west through the cover of dust, and, um, gamma radiation, anyway. They were like our navigational scrolls out there. I would like to come by and talk to you or your people again soon. Thank you for meeting me." Wow, a position statement, or a blurt, what in hell did I mean?

* * *

"Whoa Willy, got a raw spot about that poetry?"

"You know, I did write some sort of bush doggerel. I think by aiming low you can get the ball some ways into the trees. I hate those 'serious poets', who shoot off into mysticism or sentiment, and since they are the real poets, I am not, thank you."

"Hmm. Whatever you say. Willy this is very strange to me still. You are a fish in a tree here. Here! I know that is not the right saying but I still cannot believe it! So I am going to leave you for now to

49

tumble about for a couple of months maybe, get yourself some new clothes and such. I will come back and maybe take you to Umeå and Finland in a while. Just be careful of these student girls, no? Maybe find someone at Student Health to talk about your medicines every week, hold you in orbit. Or to find you a farm with cows and a big-boned daughter, eh? If I say, *Take it steady, hold it together*, that is a bit meaningless for you, no?"

Grasping his two hands, "Shit Willy, welcome to Sverige! Be well, be lucky! Ah, but you are the willy-willy!"

"Lasse, Lasse . . . Fish in a tree, that's good! I'll call you soon when, aah. . . Crikey!"

Willy sits on some steps on campus for a while, light foot traffic during class hours. He thinks back to what he left, before the stroke, sees himself mapping in light khakis, carrying a five-pound hammer with long wooden handle and map case, Brunton compass, flagging and water bottle on his belt, this same large-faced wristwatch with a precise scratch from center to twelve, by which he could gauge north by the sun within five degrees in a glance. A mapping pace calibrated to within one foot in a hundred on clear level ground. Miles of desert and mountains crunching under the feet. A broken trace of trails, soon enough erased. Perhaps little enough to lose. What vein now? Or am I just on an off-ramp of dementia?

He rides the bike out on a path through the woods, feeling a bit melancholy. Suddenly, there is a prickling in the roots of his hair, and hot and cold rippling in his ears, and he knows for ten seconds a fit is coming. He stops hurriedly and lays the bike down as the time-space crater looms; he squats so as to not fall. Sees a beetle in the grass lumbering up a bent stalk and waving antennae and rattling wings to rehearse a hop to the next blade. He follows, intently absent, tumbling into a realm of smaller things where sight and sound are amplified in a bubble but all language evaporates. Then there is a boy on a bike, stopped a safe distance off, assessing, and he is already crawling back out of that crater, picking up ragged answers to the usual questions—Where? Who am I?—before the words actually articulate those questions. Boy on bike utters an incomprehensible sound, perhaps of concern, perhaps an acronym for Just Another Foreign Entomologist, *ja fan*, and he is off. Rearranging his clothes as if disheveled by falling out of the sky, he pats his wallet and keys, takes them out, and pores over them. The boy has stopped fifty feet off, observing, and he who is still recovering Williness shouts to the other, "Which way is the town?" Yes, now he is Willy enough to come up with a word balloon, to rejoin the species, the clock, and accede to the pointed arm. He will pick up the pink bike and go there, find bearings, a stream flowing from somewhere to some here, and on. Say *fuck*, says a voice at his shoulder. What? Okay, fuck. There.

***

Lasse, driving home, thinks, *that Willy is surely different*. The one I worked with was sarcastic and brooding. Of course, this one is humbled by the language, but also, what, trying to shed, or has he actually lost some of that sarcasm. Earnest, for god's sake. No idea what he is going to do. He hasn't, nor I. He will not take to geophysics. He is, what, a child struggling to ride a bike after a head injury. Perhaps a good place for him to do that, except, well, howabout vulnerability to those student girls, damn. Glad he did not push on, wanting to hear about my home: Willy, it is a family thing, walk right in, put your feet up, conspiracy of neighbors, ghosts. The old Willy would joke it off. Saying it out loud for this new simpleton would stick it in my throat. Okay, home now?

Willy, you used to be so hard to live and work with, but funny. I did not catch on to some of the humor until lying in my cot. Now you are earnest and it is somewhat depressing. What does that mean.

***

The town has a radial plan with road and trail spokes in and out of forest, and Willy will soon be practised in "var ligger centrum", where is the center, and finding his way thence back to Flogsta, his new home. Flogsta is sixteen long towers clustered in a figure eight on thinly forested, glaciated granite on the west end of town. Each building has a central elevator with communal kitchens and a hall either side of the center with a dozen small units with bed and bath. On each roof is a sauna, actually a *bastu*, with small signs discouraging the application of water to the rocks in the heater. Southern Swedes prefer their *bastu* hotter and drier than the northerners and Finns, and it is a tossup what mode Willy will find it in; when the steam is thick the bodies are typically naked and hard to see, and voices are muffled. Actually, most often the *bastu* is empty, because his building is only half occupied yet, so Willy sits alone *waiting for Godot*, which is to say in expectation of another glancing encounter with humiliation by his alien-ness. Outside the *bastu*/sauna, there is a clear sight from Willy's new building roof to the downtown cathedral spires with their new copper cladding. Although the stars are feeble against the urban lights, the cathedral (east) shows him the way to the Big Dipper (north), so that's it, hardly the shtick of the Southern Cross, eh?

School is different, where the bungling and mangling of language is fun. There are ten people in their twenties or thirties in Willy's Swedish class. One is an Englishman, but there are eight native languages between them. The oh-so-very pleasant, perhaps not the right word, teacher Birgit does not indulge his plaintive, *sorry I know not a word*; the Liverpudlian assures him, with a rattling laugh, that nobody else here does either. Okay, get past a moment of sharp anxiety to humility. He looks about to see no-one else has a book either, we are all leaning on our ears, and suddenly he feels a bit, perhaps, deaf. I am a child in with a big group of children. See, it may not be so bad, just don't concentrate so hard you shut off the blood to ears and voice. No, by golly, it is hard to get past mistrusting the ears, seems some written text, even in another alphabet, would be easier to hang on than the hearing. Never imagined this struggle.

Birgit does have some pictures. "This is a cat. What is this, Maria Clara?" "This is . . . this is a cat." "Good, Maria Clara. And what is this, Lev?"

Lev, a Ukrainian Jew with skullcap, Maria Clara, a chubby exchange student from Costa Rica, Eva, a lantern-jawed Finn, Mahmoud, a Moroccan of angelic demeanor, Eric, the Liverpudlian redhead, Baran, a huge Kurd, Inga, an Icelander; get those others later. Inga, a slim transparent thing all the color of a puddle after rain, stared at by the others as the most exotic amongst them: Iceland! But she is gone after the second day, the explanation given for her departure obscured by a multilingual murmur of disappointment. The nationalities of each, including the lamented Inga, explained on day three with the aid of a globe. Fingers pointing by turns. Every one of them thinks, each in their own stumbling into language, what a small finger print on this globe, and I from within that print, and that spread of hands, and here we are together. Willy feels a relief that, for once, he can simply point to his origins way underneath; Eric claims Liverpool and the Beatles; Baran twiddles thumb and index finger from the Bosphorus to the Caspian, with perhaps an uncertainty about the distributaries of the Silk Road in the Middle East. For each, these capsules of indicated origins are felt as electrons of civilization, and they are all drawn to one after another Shangri La by its representative. Birgit indicated Iceland for Inga, and all regret her absence. If we are not privy to the thoughts of Birgit or the others in the class, well, let's say Willy is close to tears at this intimacy between adult strangers who have a gross of words in common, who have, as it were, thrown their clothes in the fire: and here we all are!

We have soon gotten from "This is a cat" to "Before there was one cat, and now there are two; one is black and the other white. What color is the dog, Willy?" The globe fondling was a relief of curiosities heavy in glances between them; now it is back to the blue dog. Odd, he thinks when let out in the afternoon, I do not have conscious thoughts about their method, I am just the anxious kid I probably was at age five, not getting it, listening harder, okay, struggling for the voice, trying not to look down her blouse, well, all of the time. Okay, there are differences from primary school. Willy cannot translate his own feelings round the names-in-a-hat experience with the globe, except for a helpless feeling he is in love with everyone in his class. Ensemble and in particular.

Willy tells teach in the hall in a break, "I understand you want us to immerse in Swedish. There is one thing I want to tell you in English, just in case something happens, and then we can pretend we never had the conversation. I had some neural damage a while ago, caused some seizures, you know, fuzzy bits, and while I have drugs that control them now, so far, there is a possibility one may occur, well, in class. Had one a couple days ago, less than a minute. They are not serious, brief blankness, stupidity, not grand mals or anything, nothing to be alarmed about, but just vacant. Short-term loss of memory." Good homework excuse, too, it occurs to him, should there ever be homework.

"Thank you, Willy. Some day you can tell me about it in Swedish." Spoken in Swedish, never a word of English will he hear her speak, but clearly she understood every word of his. Devilishly *snygg* butt. Thank you, Birgit, for that *snygg* word, which attaches to you so soon as given in this stream of gifts of cats, dogs, and Swedish summer. *Tack; tack tack*; thank you for the benedictions and beatitudes, don't mention it. Willy realizes the certainty that he will utter all sorts of nonsense to Birgit and the class from a compulsion to speak homage to her, coming in child-speak to first teachers from childhood everywhere. He grimaces, sort of, to think how she will report his confusions as mealtime anecdotes to her husband (mixing up *stugan* and *skogen*, cabin and forest, and *ordspråk* and *ordbok*, proverb and dictionary).

Studying the fellow students on break, he notes there are many nations, but no Asians and few blacks. No, we are about as many languages as the 747, but as white as that was dark. Okay, we are students in a student town in the northern woods. Counting the Middle East folks as white, well, not African or Asian.

***

Rolf says in English, "*Hell off a* party that was."

"Hey Rolf, how goes it with the bones?"

"The head bone's connected to the, ah, *helvete* bone."

"Jeez, I thought you guys were schnapps guzzlers, little Spanish red should have been like fruit juice."

"Willy Willy, I think I should take you home for a weekend so my dad can teach you about *brännvin*, which is to say aquavit, perhaps. Do you like to fish?"

"Ah fishing. Well, I have done some of that in several forms. Most recently trout in Tasmania with an old fart now dead, sorry to say. I taught him to pan gold in exchange for a dry fly lesson."

Oh Jock, met in a hotel dining room at what, Saint Mary's, a bit intoxicated with his cancer death sentence, and throwing up in the gold pan, peering at a trail of pink garnets leading the black heavies, and one tiny flake of actual gold. *Oh that is marvelous*! A great kick he got, too, out of my floundering ashore, coughing up a flood, after being enrolled by the river with all its dynamic load for a hundred feet. Willy thinks, I do not have friends like others but only crossings, now memories coming at me like a gust of wind's accumulation of regrets. Rolf notes the dead person in the spiel.

"Parents have a house, our house, is on a small lake, fish are, I do not know the names in English, *gädda* and carp. A person has to drink a little to keep the canoe calm."

"Hey Rolf, let me know when!" And, "Rolf? Think we ought to do another party next week, put up a sign today?"

"Do you want to be party king? That is too much money for wine."

"Just trying to get a girlfriend, you know? We'll make it BYOB: bring your own . . . How do you say 'booze'?"

***

By the second week Willy has his warm feelings for his classmates complicated by intrusions of, let's not call it reality, then, stuff, and he joins Eric in trying to nudge shyer ones into conversation, without being domineering. He is stunned to hear from Eric that Baran has told him he, Baran, has been tortured by both Turks and Iraqis, has applied for asylum here, but is not confident about getting it, and seems to be working on a mail-order Swedish bride angle. Mahmoud should speak French if he is from Morocco, no? But Willy's schoolboy French elicits only smiles and incomprehension. Maria Clara is a chubby cherub who blushes with big wide eyes at least four times a day but accepts the laughter it brings as tribute. Which side of the social wedge are you, angel? Sulky Lev has dropped out, but what "dropped out" means is a mystery.

There are more nationalities in the common room breaks, including Karelians, anyway, gotta look that up, one of whom has gathered that Willy pretends to be from Novaya Zemlya, which is actually not populated, can it be? Polar bears perhaps, and a "weather station." So, he is treated with derision until a group explanation evolves, with dubious clarification and much guttural hilarity. No, no, New Zealand. Who? Where *is* that; some other ocean. Willy finds in the public library Karelia is a push and pull region of Finland and Russia, Swedes and Finns alike anxious now to not encourage Karelian nationalism and irritate the nasty big bear. There are also forty or so Californian exchange students, college seniors, some of whom try to inveigle Willy into a trip to Munich to that Oktoberfest.

One day Eric says, "We have to go to that movie *Deep Throat*; it's showing downtown."

"What is that?"

"Linda Lovelace. You haven't heard of it?"

"Nope. I lived a sorta hermit's life last year or two, though I saw that Monterrey music festival before I left." Oh yeah, nurse told me that Janis had died before the movie even got to Perth, shit.

Eric bugs him continually, until Willy accedes, and now Mahmoud hovers, wondering what is going on.

"It is a movie. Want to come?"

"Aw jeez, Eric, it might be a bit much for Mahmoud. Hey Mahmoud, it is a crazy men and women movie, you understand?"

Beatific smile again. "Ah yes."

So, here they are on an afternoon in a movie theater with Linda Lovelace, who, frankly, gets right down to it, few puns but not actually any, shall we say, wit getting in the way as she finds her clitoris is in her esophagus. Apparently just the ticket for your average Californian male. Willy is a bit embarrassed for Mahmoud, well himself too. This is mostly rather juvenile, not that he is sure what satirical adult porn should be. Guess I'm just a bit of a prude or ignorant. Eric is gripping the back of the seat in front of him and chortling and shifting side to side. Mahmoud is at first rigid in disbelief, but then begins to rock, banging his head on his fist that rests on the seat back in front, hissing. Is this some kind of, um, religious thing, like the Hassidic in Rome airport with the phylacteries nodding out, leather thongs cutting off the blood to the scalp, itch Allah. Sorry folks, but . . . Willy sits back and punches Eric's shoulder: look at Mahmoud. Let's make sure the poor bugger doesn't explode. At last they leave together, not sure if it is really the end or just a continuous reel that has begun over again. At least the MGM lion would have kinda kept score there. Eric wants to go for a beer or six, Mahmoud not so much, smile gone ashen, seems to want to go home to brother's house, whoa, got that sister-in-law there, howabout we go walk around that historic campus and ogle the undergrads and some statuary. What, after all, do these guys do, do we each do, afternoons and all? Hang out like over-ripe fruit? Read, s'what I do, and more classes. Old Norse now, difficult until he finds Gordon, *Intro to Old Norse*, a textbook in English, in the public library, and there in that class the Swedes struggle also with the antique texts, so he has some comic relief. Should be checking math classes, but Hrafnkel riding about on Icelandic moors somehow got in the way.

***

He finds the old cemetery behind the university and botanic gardens—very quiet, with new and old trees ennobling the tidiness of granite headstones, many with runic alphabet memorials, which he copies down to decipher later. He begins to stop off in the cemetery to eat an apple and read on his way home in the afternoons, never encountering another person except the groundskeeper. I should write a letter to the city, thanking them for reserving it for me.

Sometimes he goes on along a bike path through the woods to the Norby apartment of a new friend—the American draft dodger (Willy cannot recall how they met), who plays and teaches guitar and hosts a transient motley of pot smokers—and just listens. He asks some of the other American loiterers if they know of the cemetery, but the noncommittal responses suggest the question makes him seem morbid. Several young children periodically track through the clusters of pickers and audience, rather quietly. Willy wonders if they have been continually hushed. He tries to ask a couple of them if they know, like, the Oscar Brand show, whatever it was called (Hey, got radio?). Mom listens, and waits for him to go on, kids briefly stare at him silently, and then attend to cross conversations about guitarists and Richard Nixon. But here comes one with a glass of water for him. The mom gives Willy a quizzical look, "Do you play, after all?" and passes him the current joint. Willy feels, again, like an alien in another camp of migrants, but strangely comfortable there. Nobody pays him much attention, he does not have to say who he is (a tough question), kids step over him as if he were a dog, he is allowed to sit in with a migrant family with comforting banal domestic chatter in American, and some jamming, and technical listening to a new LP or two: Clapton, Zappa, South Americans. Kids banter in English, but switch when they have a Swedish playmate guest.

"Will you go back if Nixon gives an amnesty?" he asks Mom.

58

"No, the children belong here now, and the families back there, well . . . "

"Why did you come here, rather than to say Canada?"

"It was harsh, where we came from. We wanted something completely different, a new world, not just getting away from the war. Canada was not different enough."

"Aha!" says Willy. "For me, similar, only it was the climate that rejected me. But you . . ." A child steps into her side and tugs at her sleeve. She kneels to listen, something about going to Ander's house. *OK then*. When the child slips off from under her hand, she says, "We went through nasty recriminations with my family, leaving. My two sisters took sides and have never spoken since. A lot of bitterness. And even though these children shrug it off, they feel that wreckage."

"Aha, does the good sister visit sometimes?" ventures Willy.

She laughs. Then the child is back, with another. *Anders came here because* . . .. Willy does not follow immigrant child Swedish intermixed with American, he is thrown by pitch and rhythm. She huddles with the children, so Willy goes for a pee, and when he returns everyone has gone into a back room to watch TV news, so he thinks maybe he ought to leave them to go about their business, anyway.

***

PBC number 2. Fewer people, initially, too much chicken, but there is beer and *brännvin*. Willy, Stefan the Pole, and Andrei the Greek have learned a bit more Swedish, and try pieces of it out on each other. Willy hams it with elements from the materials they have all seen, each in their different classes, now that books have been issued: *Bussen nummer 9 hittar på andra sidan av vägen*, and *Kerstin Skjöld är sjuksköterska*, the last a lovely gob sluicer throwing the foreigners in the deep end of shwoolsh. Laughter and more *brännvin*, and hall neighbors begin to exchange gesticulations and language breccia, who have not previously spoken more than a greeting, *Hej*!

"But what are you really doing here, Willy?" asks Elsa. She did not hear Lasse explain this on his behalf last week.

"I had a stroke in the outback, suffered some neuro damage, am taking some time to recuperate, and reassess what to do next."

"But why here? It is, shall we say, unusual."

"Yes, most other down-unders go to that London. I'm not good at following the lead." Actually I am a solitary prospector from the back side of the black stump, socially suspect, unreliable. Have an unarticulated antipathy for that London, hard to say why. Grandfather, a survivor of Passchendale, had intense hatred of all things English. And, of course, the Boche.

"Did you come in a plane through München?"

"Through Frankfurt."

"Have you seen or heard the news from München?"

"No, the TV news is a bit past me yet. The Olympics, yes? I think the cousins took the eights rowing as expected, but I didn't see it."

"Oh, but there is a big hostage situation, you have not heard? Some people from Palestine have taken captive most of the Israeli team."

This takes some time to get purchase. "Hostages."

"We should go watch the nine o'clock news," says Elsa.

He is not quite cleaned up in the kitchen but leaves others to finish and goes to the basement rec-TV area with Elsa and Josef. The Olympics news is that Israeli hostages and gunmen were killed in helicopters at an airport, after a PLO attack and stellar West German bungling. The numbers of Palestinians dead and escaped, and hostages killed, are yet to be confirmed. Much of the reporting is in English, but through layers of quotes and commentary he gets that the TV knows bugger all. Bewilderment, then indignation subsiding into *Aw shit, people.*

Israel, Palestine; another mess. Where Willy grew up, Jews were invisible. Only after crossing the water did he ever wonder if any of those in his boys' high school might have been Jewish. An assembly of 1100 supposedly protestant high school boys singing "Rejoice, rejoice, Immanuel, shall come to thee oh Israel." No Arabs, anyway.

Somebody told him, in about 1971, one of his old geology classmates, Ben G, was in Sydney and moldering in a depression in a brick suburb, and Willy, *en route* to or from a molybdenum prospect in the New England ranges, sought him out. Found him killing time, headed soon to a scholarship in groundwater with the famous-in-his-field Jacob Bear in Haifa. And wearing the thing: a yarmulke.

"Haifa? Jeez, Ben, what's up with that?" Pointing at the yarmulke.

Grinned, blue eyes throwing a sparkle of amusement, "I know you knew but would not acknowledge 'the Jewish thing.'" While sinking into a floral discomfort of a couch, dismal black tea provided by the landlady, putzing through the polite conversation somebody might think owed to a visitor.

"Hey, it's just fluids in partial differential equations. Don't drink it if you don't like it," said Ben. Lost my grip on time and space there, thought Willy, pre-war couch and mildew, and the Hebrews and hypercalculus conspiring, in a Sydney brick suburb.

"Okay, I confess to my complete and efficient ignorance. I dunno which is worse: the math or the militant, silly hat?"

Tried to get him out for a beer, with landlady's encouragement, she anxious about Ben's "morbidity." He just went out, supposedly to the toilet, did not come back. Humiliation, then. That was before the stroke, and, yes, humiliation wounded more then. I said to the woman, "Of course, I'm just a yob, but he mighta . . . " Ben, old friend I thought; evidently we did not connect in the root zone.

Standing leaning on a column in the rec area watching the Munich thing on the TV, Willy flashes on that old humiliation by Ben between the hardly informative TV journalist spiels, and suddenly dissolves. Bloody hell, the world is too grim to give a shit about my one-time humiliation, so trivial, and getting a bit teary with it. Shit!

Elsa sees the tears, touches his arm. "Are you Jewish, Willy?"

"No no. Not really." Some amusement at obfuscation regarding his origins. Elsa will report to Jim and others that Willy has an emotional side, that he wept for the Munich victims, and might be part-Jewish.

Willy feels the emotive heat subside into sorrowful troughs for a couple minutes, then back to where-the-hell-am-I disorientation until Elsa takes his hand briefly, says she is going, thank you. Okay, I will come with you.

***

Next day the class is sitting before Birgit's arrival and Willy goes to the blackboard, takes a piece of chalk, clears his throat for attention.

"I want to give us all a word," he says.

"Yesterday I needed this word and could not find my little word book, so I had to go ask my neighbor what it is. So now I will tell you this word."

He takes the chalk and slashes a sloping line across the board, and at the lower right end he writes *vanliga,* ordinary. "Let this line be

62

everyday".

Then he draws a closed circle above the line, in the middle. "And inside this line, we shall say, is 'out of the everyday'. In English we say, *extra-ordinary*, or in english English, 'extrordinary', a clumsy word but hear how it goes egg-STROR-dinary, de-Dum-di-di-dee, and the sound gives it special meaning. I asked my friend the Swedish word and he said, *extraordninär*, which I thought is a bit, ah, well, and he said also *märkvärdig*, remarkable, a bit ordinary I thought?

"So here we all are, and remember the globe, how we all pointed to where we came from, oooh and aah, last year we were all in very different places, good or not so good for us, but because we are all together like children in this place it is very special, *extrordinär*. Unless one of us has a better word in their own language, so please tell us what yours is, each one."

Birgit has entered and stands quietly just inside the door, listening. Willy sucks in his own audacity and waggles his hands in embarrassment. There is no way out of this stream but through.

"So Birgit works here, she has had other classes before us and will have others, perhaps we could say it is her job, and ordinary for her. But."

Willy steps toward the class and gestures, and steps back and swipes a break in the circle and draws a seagull squiggle in the break. "Because she comes into this *extrordinär* place with us, and is our angle, I mean angel, in this place, she too."

Now he has lost his footing altogether, and lunges to his chair, bejazzus I am a clod. Birgit comes in and brushes his shoulder with fingertips, and with faintest smile says, "I am very privileged to be with all of you, in fact an *extrordinär* class."

Oh! the class beams with sentiment, *Si si extraordinario,* says Maria Clara, and everybody goes to write their own word, and Willy is a bit disappointed the bloody Romans seem to have staked the ground in so many languages, we will have to ask Eva, Baran and Mahmoud to spell out and explain the roots of their own words.

Willy is wondering how she will regain control of the class when she says, "I have a small announcement, I will get details next week, but the school is taking all its classes on a bus tour to Stockholm in two weeks. It will be a slightly longer day, I hope you can all make it. We will go to the Riksdag and see the government in session, and see the Queen's Palace and a number of other things."

But, Willy thinks. It really is *extrordinär,* we are all building a new language together, and new identities, those with families or religion a bit constrained, in this classroom we are equals without politics, sometimes animals cringing together in a corner of a corral it feels, not a flock but an assembly of disparates. A sudden chill as he is pierced by recollection of a night passed in shearer's quarters at a woolshed, where a few hundred ewes and lambs had just been separated, and cried all night to each other through the pens. Willy puts his head in his hands, and Birgit gives him a longer-than-customary look. Shit mon, soon we will be driven out, and I will have to become something. As soon as one says this is *extrordinär,* the future glares through the boards, and I am not any closer to that something. Peter Piper tricked out in a prickly suit not sympathetic to its wearer. Go out and squeeze a tear over the rail at Fyris Ån where there is usually a smoker pulling a calming breath out of the coffee-mill scented air, perhaps.

***

One Monday there are a handful of what he gathers are Cubans in the common room, and a couple Russians. The Russians are shabbily dressed thugs, zek orphans he thinks, they might be students of Hollywood noir; the Cubans are earnest young men leaning in to murmur in low voices. Willy in jest raises a fist and says, "Viva Che!", and is relieved none of them seem to have heard him. One of the Russians bellows at him, "Where you from?" with a western movie accent. And the Karelian two tables removed from both says "Novya Zemlya!", and goes over to the Russians to explain the joke. Guffaws, again. Willy cannot read the dynamics of this exchange, he is amused at the Novaya Zemlya recirculating but the Karelian is neither humble not defiant, exactly, the Cubans are impatient at the interruption. Boy oh boy, thinks Willy, who is gonna be on the bill next in this wild west show? So much for this being a sleepy student town.

Russians and Cubans fraternizing now, what are they hatching? Slo-mo migration of revolution following Cuban missile crisis into some tropical corner (Cubans don't like the cold). Africa?

Just two days of that lot and they disappear again. On the second day one of the Russians going by slaps Willy on the shoulder and says something guttural, and they all laugh. Willy smiles and wonders how it would go if they all turned up at a PBC party. They look at the Californian exchange students like wolves seeing poodles outside the cage.

***

A few days after the Cubans have gone he is sitting alone, reading, in the school lounge in a break when a thirty-ish American sidles in, mind-if-I-sit-here sort of manner, and asks where he is from. Oozing disingenuousness.

"Novaya Zemlya, some think."

"What I heard, Australia."

"Hmmmm."

"So, how do you feel about all these bourgeois Americans. Don't they take the cake?"

"Aw, nah." Willy puzzles thickly over this awkward customer—geez, there are some oddballs in and around this school crowd. "Are you maybe their security detail?" Meaning the Californian exchange student group.

"No no, just waiting for someone!"

"You don't look like a waiter."

The guy grabs the back of a chair and leans in to give an icy stare.

"Sorry," says Willy. "I got kicked by a cowgirl in the etiquette a while back and my couth was dislocated."

"What the hell, man. I'm just trying to make conversation!"

"No," says Willy, "I know what you are; you're a spook." And thinks, that shy mumbler I used to be got left behind somewhere, crikey.

"What's your name kid."

"Kid, is it! Wouldn't you rather hang with the Cubans over there?" Actually they are not there this week; right.

"A smart ass!" Spook stands. Doesn't have the stature to exactly loom menacingly, seems cool enough, however, to select "defuse" mode, and moves out across the lounge to the double doors, which happen to be locked, fumbles with the I-knew-that act and disappears stage left.

***

Willy buys a small radio, thinking, oh you know, background, osmotic absorption of the rhythm of the language, the rhythm he fails to hear through at times. He finds there are just three stations on this radio with limited hours, and, bizarrely, all three seem to play accordion music a lot of the time: *dragspel* indeed. Perhaps he will inquire about a shortwave radio, which might bring in a station from farther afield, that Europe should be just off a little, no? Already he cannot recall where he bought this radio, or if there were others. Lot of the streets are indistinct and the people all tend to dress alike, except for a few oddments among the foreign students, including himself. Willy has stepped into a clothing store, and bolted out again, mumbling over the shoulder at the cash register.

***

He tries reading Dostoyevsky's "Idiot" again, in the town library, high school the last time. He does not remember it well. But he is exasperated at the thorny tangle of Russian names, and of course Dostoyevsky cannot report on the contents of his grand mal seizures any more than Willy can his absences; there is just a resetting of the character, of time, and perhaps the subsequent reset bestows a kind of innocence, which strikes those around as a kind of nobility. Forgive him whatever, he did not intend whatever, and he has forgotten it anyway. But Myshkin's saintliness is his own, anyway, not a Christian pietism like that of Dostoyevsky's other *tragic* Russians. So Willy skip-reads up to Myshkin's final collapse at the deathbed of the great courtesan, and reads that chapter three times. Ugh: three aspirin and goodnight.

Not that the seizures are such tribulations, he tells someone, you find yourself on a strange street, hopefully not run over, and you go to the corner, there will be a sign, Drottningsgata perhaps; look at watch: *how-much-is-the-clock*; or you ask *where is the town center*, and there you are; and shortly you remember your name, and that pink bike is yours, yes, that pink is very helpful.

When Myshkin comes around after a fit he will not have learnt anything new beyond the reset; the maneuvering and cruelty of the world is unabated, he has to stand and grasp a door handle and hear an accounting of the damage inflicted, the humiliation he is expected to take on, though of course the serf class will have cleaned up the vomit.

***

Bruce mate

"Well here we are." Where you may send willy-nilly under extravagant flourish of your royal postage what you will of southern gnus, your research into the late Mack of our fraternal order of prospectors, and your quests among the Imperial MacAllens of Three Rivers or others, and the sun-bit dust between. In exchange for this brief report on topsy turvy land and the strangeness of gravity therein.

I'm buggered if I know actually how it is going. It's like one of those impressionist French movies with plot TBD, to be determined, peut etre. There, I'm already leaking out suppressed buggers and bloodies. Crikey.

I could have been floppish wrack on the coast of Montevideo or Trieste but here we are. It is cool mossy forest over glaciated granite with Viking middens poking through the curtains, but also a student town. My Swedish class is a cluster of political refugees from half the 36 corners of the earth, with occasional conspiratorial waves of Russians and Cubans, and even the CI bloody A, eh! Slew of US draft dodgers and exchange students, too.

The other thing. Drugs are supposed to suppress the brain farts, mostly working, some side effects like irregular stupidity such as even you would remark. A full flip-out the other day: a gal asked if I would look at her bark paintings to say if they were authentic or something, and she had a solitary goldfish in a bowl, and I was snagged by the bowl lensing and undular rippling in place and zoned out, and she highly offended (I realized afterward) at my ignoring her, and then panicked that I was in a coma (!) for a mo. I think some of these drugs are residua from production of a new formula for say malaria, and they think, What could we market this for then, rather than flushing it into the ocean and killing all the fish.

Another odd thing: I have several times now done the peanut butter chicken thing as a party in the communal kitchen, 25-ish people at the last one; I have become an extrovert on days without an "S" in them, which I do not understand myself. Saturday does not have an S here: its name means bath day, *hardly more bizarre than Saturn's day.*

There is a lot of strange stuff here that stops me in my tracks. So close to Russia, and they have a huge air force, and there are sudden long wide spots in forest highways to serve as random airstrips, so the cold war is on simmer just up the road. If you ask about them, they shrug.

To sum up, I'm buggered if I know, but it is interesting. Let me know what you find about Macs and Mack. And keep stocked up on hot patches, yer bugger: I know you drive over those stakes to show off, and I could see you fixing a puncture on Hay Street (the Perth one) to impress that Mac.

Lasse came down for a day. In fact it was he who prompted the first PBC party. Strange to see him here, at home, not the field assistant working "our plan". I used to think he preferred to work with you, the more rational one, but he said he found me "entertaining," perhaps like the sightings of platypus in Tasmania. He, Lasse, took me to meet the geophysics prof. They do most science classes in English here it turns out; but I was intimidated, morbidly. Perhaps after I find some footing. I do not understand what Lasse is up to, or if he knows himself, perhaps he is taking over his old music school. He whistles and hums to inhabit another world, and when he pulls out his harmonica, well, you know it.

Did I ever tell you about his picking up that tiger snake and crooning at it, mad bastard, hard to believe now. I'll go visit him soon, just a few hours on a train, when I get a grip.

The bit about the girl with the fishbowl in the letter to Bruce was apocryphal crap, of course, but it was shorthand for the flavor of this life, up to the present. Things are . . . well, humorous.

***

Right, he determines, need physical tune-up. No martial arts in the phone book (but what would it be called?). Or big punch bags in student nations gyms. In the pines outside his apartment block he finds a tree with a handy branch and does chin-ups, push-ups and sit-ups on the ground, and runs a few miles on the bike trail. Then he finds a three-inch birch a few yards off the pine, which he wraps his shirt around to be a *makawara* post to pound with fists. He gives up the tree-punching after a couple of times, feels a bit silly—Hey, someone will probably see, and report me for abusing the birch—but he keeps up the rest in a desultory way. In his undergrad days in Wellington he went to a small studio in the back of a commercial building, where a sullen Okinawan sensei, with hands deformed by punching posts and boards and rice bags, held lessons, endless block-block-counter drills and a few *katas*. It was a cheerless routine, with humiliations at his inflexibility, at being constantly out of step with the other students, and whacked with *shinai*: split bamboo swords. The sensei said, Must not pull punch, no difference real and training, always real, Go, Stop, no halfway. He had to drag himself to it and was addicted to it. How did he abandon it for so long? Oh, very easily. But now the urge drags him out of bed at the crack of dawn to run a bit in noisy trail-slapping shoes, and sneak off to his tree to huff, puff, and rehearse the drills, restraining the *kiai*! to a *tseh* . . . to avoid descent of an emergency response. He has a mental block on the last *kata*, repeats over and over up to the blockage. The body should remember if the mind does not, dreams will coach him, yes? Dreams decline, so far. The mind keeps evading itself. How does that *kata* go? What does it mean that he cannot break this blockage? I do not own the *kata* and it disavows me. Aw, let's just get depressed then.

Early, the beautiful Birgit, his Swedish teacher, says, pointing to his scabby knuckles, "What is it with your hands, Willy? One hand could be an accident, two is a problem."

He shrugs in embarassment. "Ah it is a little . . .karate thing . . . In the trees . . .just exercise you know?" She is his teacher, he is called on the mat. No I am not a tough guy, I am a klutz. Wait, did her fingertips brush my elbow while I stared at the floor, before she walked off? No no no.

Punch through the little problems. *Tseh* becomes *hejah*! Then, yes, a head comes around the trees to his stomped-flat seclusion, stares exchanged, it is a mushroomer or something, small salute, then gone.

***

A day or so later a face pops in through the trees with the first spears of sunlight, and Stefan the Pole enters his "clearing," catching him mid-*kumite*. "Phsss . . ." He fades, flaps palms on thighs, and gives Stefan a wee bow. Stefan gives a friendly puzzling nod and approaches.

"What are you doing, Willy."

"Some little thing from karate of Okinawa, which I learnt too long ago, ja, and some, hup." Pointing to the now somewhat polished branch, steadying his breathing.

"I also, some judo," says Stefan, wiping jogger's sweat on his forearm.

"Jaha!" They regard one another grinning.

"Hej." Stefan offers handshake, which Willy takes defensively in two hands. Stefan stoops slightly, spins on one heel, and swoops Willy's hand high, his other hand grip is undone, the twist is cocked and the pose for the throw held, conceded by Willy's slap on his own thigh.

"Aha! *Très bien*! Once again now . . ."

Wrists engage now, classic judo grapple, feet shuffle. Willy breathes deeply to fake a rhythm, lunges to grab Stefan's left forearm with his left hand and pulls it back under the right, and when Stefan's grip breaks he reverse-punches underneath. Whap, punch stopped on the rib cage. Now Stefan steps back flushed, says, "Altså! One for the other!" They glow at each other, mixed respect and hand-flapping language awkwardness. Although each has been in the same Swedish school going on a fortnight, they are not in the same class and their vocabularies have been developing along different threads.

"Willy, why do you do this?"

"Er, it was just when I was in school, you know, like a sport." Flexing the arms. "And you?"

"It was in the army."

"So it is not just good guy over the bad guy, right?"

"Yes, no, it is you and the other."

"Just so, whether we are right or wrong."

"Man must be able to believe in himself, then he is the good guy."

"That can be difficult in, shall man say, the army?"

They shuffle a bit.

"It is hard to talk like a child. About judo and karate and, ah," says Stefan.

"And the meaning of life." Both laugh. Somehow each knows the other also feels the words amusingly on the loose, like dogs pulling on leashes, but that under the muddle is something, or things, they would be hard put to articulate in their native tongues.

"But it is easier for me because most of these know some English. How do you do it?"

"My professor is from Poland. There are, of course, some other Polish. Some political, some not."

"Yes."

"I am both. Mostly not political, just scientist, but I said some stupid things." Laughs. A long gaze between them. Then Stefan gives a small wave and is quickly gone, footsteps fading down the gravel path.

Willy is slightly dizzy. He is thankful for the conversation, but swings from gratitude to wistfulness to dissatisfaction with himself. He jumps up to the branch, hangs there five seconds, does five chin-ups angrily, another ten feeling the ridiculous foreigner, and then gradually comes back into his skin as the shoulders begin to shudder and say, That's all! To hell with you, then, shoulders, let's go to pushups. And . . . Quivering. Stop counting then. Go, go, and . . .

***

Two days later the spook meets him at the bicycle rack when he arrives at school.

"Listen," the spook says.

"Say, are you the same guy from couple days ago over there, or do you all just look alike?"

Ignores that. "Some of the foreigners in this town are persons of interest in various international goings-on. You are close to a couple of them, here where you live and in your classes, and there are others in this school. I know you also hang out occasionally with that draft dodger, the guitarist, we're not so interested in him, but some of the other occasionals . . . I'm not asking you to spy, just to keep your ears open, and let me know if you get a hint of anything dire."

"Kinda like, if I hear of a plot to attack the Israelis in Munich, I should give you a heads up?"

"Oh, you are so swift."

"Well, I would feel more secure to hear you are busy protecting the Free World against the threats of yesterday than if you are dreaming up new stuff. Hey, and who are these guys I'm supposed to know, who are, as you say, what, 'suspects'?"

"Rather not prejudice your dealings with anyone. I'm just saying, keep your ears open. Quite a few people have come to your parties. I could actually contribute to your wine fund."

"Jesus, Curl, stay away from my— How did you even find out about our, our parties? And, too, why am I not a 'suspect' myself, eh? Yeah, not in your jurisdiction."

"I don't know a lot about you yet, but I will if I need to. You are too much of a confrontational prick to be exactly suspicious. All I'm asking is, be alert. I have an office in the American Express place on Fyris Torg, next to the Cathedral, case something turns up."

Jesus, he thinks as he throws a leg over the bike and pushes into the street, I've been, what, *contacted*. How do you wash that off? And how do I sit in class and look them in the eyes and forget about it? Thanks for that shot of paranoia, bastid.

* * *

That night he rides the bike out to the mounds of the esker people, as he thinks of them now, in old Uppsala, and finds a cranny under whispering pines, rolls out a towel on pine needles, doffs his Swandry hooded pullover coat and lays down to sleep, or entertain the spirits of the place. He has discovered *The Golden Bough* in the library, where Old Uppsala figures in several ur-history references. Though it seems Old Uppsala and the mounds are only maybe third century CE. They are still immigrants compared to the Australians, I mean the aborigines. Must have hung out losing the melanin in that Ukraine for a few millennia out of Africa. Lacking Swedenborgian susceptibilities, he goes to sleep on his side, lulled by susurrus of breeze in trees, before being stirred by a couple of police.

Apparently alerted by someone spotting moon-glint on bicycle. He is slow to surface, the stars are all wrong, whasat, he has no papers on him and struggles to explain what in hell a weirdly dressed foreigner with pink girl's bike is doing sleeping on the graves of the ancients. What indeed. The cops drive him, bike in boot, back to his apartment building, where he digs out passport with its stamps for them. Stefan is up in the kitchen, slightly uneasy about the cops. Willy explains, and somehow it is easier than with the cops. Sleeping out is not necessarily diabolic for Stefan, quizzical about it being at the mounds. Hey, he is a scientist, and whether catholic or communist in the life he fled, he has put that mythic shit aside. The police politely leave them. Should be the opportunity for asking Stefan more about what his story is, so far just the guarded and peremptory here-we-all-are. Willy thinks about confiding about the spook—you know, it's us against them—but he's actually a bit spooked by the spook, consciousness of his own alien-ness confounding his judgment.

He misses sleeping under the night sky. Waking on narrow cot, gobful of stars always startling, intuitively checking rotation, a hand span, say, until dawn, then a long stare, dream sediments trickling down a wedge of heaven, until nodding off, as if in a symphony hall.

***

PBC number three, ten days after the last. Two dozen people, many of whom he has never met, some even from outside the complex. Not enough booze, but some go off to get more at systemet, the state liquor store. Party overflows the kitchen and down the hall; that's okay, every resident of this end is here. Except Morsdottir, the smoker.

Rolf says, "I saw her leaving earlier."

"Maybe she has a date," speculates Willy.

"She was a little gruff," says Rolf. "Did you piss her off?"

"Aw, gee."

"Willy, did you damnit get in her teenaged pants?"

"No! But . . . "

Party is big enough he is not the star anymore, he is just the cook, so nobody is paying attention to Rolf's "But what?"

"But the mother," says Willy sheepishly. Jesus, that Rolf is suddenly a Big Brother, bristly, stiff.

Two days ago, mother turned up, daughter not in, so chatting in kitchen while Willy made tea. Chatting! She asked Willy—no, told him—he was doing these parties because he was lonely, took him a bit to get that "*ensam.*" Willy was caught off guard, momentarily speechless. He had been struggling with some Elder Edda and his voice had been stuck in a wrong track. Whoa, and what about you, Dottirsmor, and thy silent, depressed smoking daughter, I am blushing I feel. He had stepped up to hear her better, accent from a different quarter, maybe Skåne, he thinks, so when she turned from the sink they were face to face. So bam! There it happened, off to the races, two lonelies shuffle-sprinted down the hall to his room as he wondered what code he had failed to read. Wavelet rolling weathered sticks up a beach, in moonlight, happens two roll over one another. That is *ensamheten* undone. "Oh!" she cried. *Thy back will crack or I cry that, John Anderson, my Jo.* Willy let her use the bathroom first, and as she went out she touched his knee through the sheet and said "Tack", and the weight of his, ah, unworldliness settled like dusk.

"She only looks boney," offers Willy to Rolf timidly, "but . . . I don't think she'll be back for me. You know she *is* only forty or so."

Rolf fixes him with a now-you-listen-to-me glare, then says, "Willy, this next weekend is my mother's birthday. There is a small party with some interesting uncles. I would like you to come; we can do the fishing thing."

"Err right. What do I need?"

He has prepared the peanut butter sauce ahead this time, so there is less flailing in the wok initially, and some who seem very attentive to what he is doing, trying to figure a recipe and make mental notes, are disappointed, but then he does a fried rice which gets them excited again.

"What are you doing? You cannot fry the rice before you boil it!"

"But yes I can! Makes it nutty."

When the rice is opalescent, he puts it in water to boil while he fries up a mix of odd Nordic vegetables, flailing again with spatula and sizzling of oil, more oil, and again. Scandinavian salad slaves are fascinated by the quantities of oil, not just deep frying but actually going into the food, smoking up the kitchen, carrying degenerate odors over the party and the whole wing. Spices bought by the nose whose names he does not know ride like, how do you say, Valkyries, and someone else is knocking at the door.

"So, why did you leave Australia?" a new, freckled face asks at his elbow. Braid of red hair across the top of the head, sorta Ukrainian Willy thinks, or that Sylvia Plath look. Hey babe.

"Ah, we broke up, perhaps. I had a religious experience in the desert and needed to recover, and now I am going to do geophysics in grad school here." Twice a day, should write my replies down to show evolution.

"Will you go home?"

"Oh, I'm not from Australia, you know." Ah, it is not really funny, perhaps perverse, to be a puzzle.

A weird diminutive American, dressed in orange and yellow Haight Ashbury garb, tugs at his elbow and seems to be interested in selling Willy a self-published picture book relating to a dialog of Plato. Afterwards, Willy will wish he had maybe promised to buy one, but in the throng he is distracted—What a weirdo—and, anyway, he is sort of trying to keep track of Freckles here, so he groans something disparaging about old Greek fascists.

"No feeling for the origins of philosophy," murmurs Haight Ashbury.

"Australians are oafs, I am an oaf, but I am only part Australian."

The Platonist turns to go, and Willy says apologetically, "I used to have an opinion on, ah, Plato, but that was in another hemisphere."

He is surprised at his own accidental pun, but they are both gone, he is unheard. Pissin' in the wind. He has a drop, declining toward abject humiliation. But that's humility with a whimper, right? He wishes Freckles would let him whimper a little, close up, be a kissing confessor.

Okay, he tells two or three people who insist on a recipe for PBC, as he throws the chicken in the sauce and then serves. "Boil the chicken in pieces, as you see, as big as your big toe. Melt peanut butter carefully in this pan, if it burns just a little, no problem, goes dark, adding peanut oil to thin it, then basil, cayenne, and a little cheap sherry. Not too much sherry, it will get too thick, and keep adding oil and warming until it is dark and, um, will just drop from the spoon. There it is."

Baran and a Swedish gal as generously built as he is turn up. It's a new wife, they seem to be in lust. Jesus, like mare and stallion having crashed the wall between stalls, married in haunch, hock, and withers, Percheron scale. Lots of ho-ho-ho. Willy asks her name but does not get it, ear is still not tuned to hear through some agglomerations of consonants. Kinda loud already, here.

A bit later some newcomer remarks that Willy has an accent, and he is flattered that the person intimates he has a grasp of the language with just a bit of not-quite-so in the vowels, but then he realizes they mean his vowels do not fit any pattern the person recognizes, and is deflated. Humiliated again, lacking the grace or whatever it is for humility. Up then down. Ooo errr. Better go see that ex-army nurse, *studentsköterskan,* about this sloshing mood. Sister of whatsit, Katie, isn't it? Sisters of take-this-and-gawn-get-outa-here. Ought to draft those gals to run the UN.

The nurse will tell him to try Vitamin B. Or is it D? No matter, probably placebo, get one of each in case I have to look her in the eye again and say, Yes, I got those.

***

On a cloudy afternoon he rides to the cemetery and, pulling in, turns his head at a raucous robin flying from curb to tree, hits a cobble awry and bumps the curb, feet abandon pedals and splay to brace, and he falls on hip and shoulder, rolling with the pink sudden disconformity of bicycle twisting over him: hmph! He sits attendant upon whatever humor might choose to settle. Hath thrown a wobbly! he mutters, assessing. Finds sprocket has scraped a leg greasily, chain is thrown, fumbling at which begrimes his fingers. Who saw, anyone? An older woman on a path inside the cemetery, slow-walking, here like him for sober leafy sanctuary turning colors, or to say Hej to great grandpa, disequilibrated by immigrant un-balletics, looking, turning away. Aah! Kicks front wheel, rub-rub it spins, untrue but not so badly as to prevent. Madam, would you be so good as to describe how it went, arse over kettle? I did not myself have time for an objective narrative, and now, begrimed and head-bumped, well, verily, where in hell was I going? Robin above clucks, Tut-tut-tut. Oh yes, we're off to see the wizard, over the rainbow the first leg, get my marbles back, that's it.

***

In a brief, wet, early snow he rides the bike out to the guitarist's, alone on dark bike path in hushed woods, sitting upright and hypnotized by the huge flakes. He knocks, enters, shakes off his coat, and sits against the wall with snow melting into his hair. No surprise shown at his coming. Why can he not remember their names? Two tuning guitars together give him a barest glance. He gathers they are talking about another picker who is deeply into heroin, they have about given up on him, a sister is coming from the US to try to corral the pieces, they are obliged but reluctant to engage with her, and replay the disintegration and betrayals. Wife of the house (is it Beck?) comes in and puts a face towel on Willy's wet hair with a pat. Hi! She says she hears the junkie is squatting in a unit in Flogsta now, and Willy says, "Heck, that's where I live, should I check up on him?" Even in English now the words fall out unbidden and volunteer him for, um, what is it he's getting into? Bloody hell, Willy, you have zero social skills.

The players look at him as if at a Christian who has volunteered to go to the forest to check on the welfare of a man-eating tiger: Sure!

Willy asks them, out of the blue, "Did the CIA bother you, here I mean?"

Some give him a sharp look. Willy tells them about the spook, and they listen patiently, but without emotion.

"Ah yes but it was minimal, for us. They seemed to accept we were done, had relinquished it all."

Perhaps, thinks Willy, the spook was just going through random motions, not about Helsinki or the Cubans or Munich or these folk. Certainly I can hardly believe he was real.

"I should just forget about that guy," he says, "but it felt sordid, you know? He invited me to visit him in an office at American Express."

"Uh-huh."

Willy feels confused these draft dodgers are not infuriated at even the mention of the CIA in these north woods. As he bikes home to

Flogsta in the dark the confusion becomes anger, at whom he is not certain. Perhaps if the spook were a *normal* person, say a geologist less than half tropo, or a guy in a bank, one might exchange courtesies, but . . . Whoa! A fox, is it, loping blackness, runs across the trail, and a spurt of excitement, goddamn! goddamn! admiration for the fox dispelling the funk.

Willy does go to the particular Flogsta building where the junkie is supposed to be when he gets back, but is relieved when a resident—an east European with poor Swedish—tells him, *Gone.* Police, ambulance, gone! Relieved, but a feeling of failure creeps like the grass emerging from the fast-melting snow. His mood drops again and worsens as he picks at it in irritation. Having not succeeded in his mission (to do what, godammit?), and sickened at the acceptance of the CIA, he thinks he will not be able to go back to the guitarist's.

***

Chapter 5  Darlana

Rolf drives Willy up to the family home in Dalarna on Friday afternoon. Willy is speechless at the symphony of woods and lake land, with houses and barns red, orange and green, but mostly *Falu red*, says Rolf, and funny old houses with the second floor projecting over the lower floor in the eaves and gables. Rolf's woodchopper Saab rockets like a horse that knows its way and is given its head, sounding off as if it may be some years since it was road-legal.

Little settlements on some of the lakes look like summer camps. Rolf confirms most are. "It is very overgrown, even since I was young. Used to be many more small farms under those trees." They have settled into the conversational mode that is habitual in their apartment hall, in which Willy speaks Swedish and Rolf English, which is somewhat strained over the Saab noise, and it is hard to know if either is clear what they are talking about, precisely.

The red house and inevitable barn, linked, asserted against the forest. Rolf says, "Kitchen dining in the house, bedrooms and living in the old barn." And other buildings clustered like a brood of chickens from the house to the small lake, one of which is his dad's ironworks shop, says Rolf. Buildings could be twenty or two hundred years old, thinks Willy, will ask later.

"You mean a blacksmith's shop? A smithy, in English."

"Yeah. Used to be a stable, a horse barn, and he bought the equipment from a horseshoe place, and all over the district.

"That damned lake," says Rolf, "not so big, but it has few fishermen, and there are some big *gädda* in there—your pike—that have been on the hook several times and ask politely about your grandmother before they bite through your hand and leap back into the deep."

"*Jo!*" Willy sees that the lake and forest are the bed of Rolf's youth.

"Mother's car. I like to ask her why she hides it down there."

"Hides? Why?"

"Oh, she works at the hospital in Stockholm in the week and has an apartment there. Lots of couples in these Olaf Palme times pretend to live separately to avoid family tax. The government sends people to see if your car is parked at the house of your ex-wife and such, and if it is, you get fined on top of the tax."

"Some, ah, peculiarities about this country, oodle ardle awdle. Hey, what's that beast next to the shop? Looks like a Russian Land Rover!"

"That there is Far's Volvo Lapplander, 1960-ish army surplus, his work 'truck.' It is indeed a beast, but the sister and I both learned to drive in it."

Lost in his appraisal of this machine, Willy misses the mention of the sister.

Rolf parks in the loop at the end of the drive, outside the smithy, which has an open sliding door and an inviting deep dimness.

"We will probably stay in the boat house there. The uncle with the Mercedes there will be in the main house."

"Come on. They will all be out on the lake side. If you need to piss after that drive, there is a toilet there." They enter the smithy, perform the necessaries, and go through the dim-lit shop with smells of iron slag, past anvil and forge with racks of tools and semi-ordered piles of steel in various degrees of evident intent.

"Aah!" whispers Willy. It is a working shop, full of ageless, undifferentiated magic and slough.

An old bloodhound with grey muzzle comes to greet Rolf, they knock heads, and Rolf blows in his nostrils. "Hey Fram!" Fram gives Willy a quick sniff, laboriously turns in the narrow passage, and leads them out to the lakeside door, sweeping the floor with his tail.

Four people in canvas-backed iron chairs are sitting in the doorway, in dappled shade of birch trees, looking over the lake. There are several bottles, empty and full, on a small table, and a big plate with a few crumbs. The cool of the smithy, its iron breath and the palpable musical rest between ringing and pounding, is at their backs. Although Mor has just arrived, Far has been playing host for some hours, it seems, and the three men are slightly louder than sober. Several smelly candles are burning to discourage mosquitoes, in case.

General introductions, with backslapping from the "Dutch contingent." Frans is Mor's brother, who lives near Amsterdam with partner Joost. They appear delighted to have another foil for their rattly wit, Mor (Adela), having just got home, lagging their intake and ebullience, and Willy feels how Rolf is glad to have a buffer for the duffers; he is quick to pour Willy and himself a glass each of the stuff from one of the bottles: *brännvin*, Willy sees. "*Skål!* Let the lesson begin!" he adds, to general amusement. Far (Bengt) laughs and smacks a small gong above the door with a broomstick, without getting up.

"So you speak Swedish, Willy?" asks Adela.

"Slightly. It gives the friends at Rolf's and my residence laughs," says Willy.

"Well, he does okay," says Rolf, "for a three-week beginner, but it is a wonder that he can ask a woman in the post office for postage stamps without being arrested!"

"Ahem. I think this *brännvin* may help," offers Willy.

"Well, we speak a lot of English now," says Bengt, "because this Joost has no Swedish more than *ja ja, tack*."

Rolf has somehow concealed up to now a gift for Adela, which he presents with a kiss. While she opens it—something in crystal from Örrefors and chocolates—Bengt relates that Frans has lived with Joost since the war. They met in Colditz Castle.

"What is it, candlesticks?" asks Adela, giving Rolf a peck, and a poke in the ribs with a long finger.

"Maybe just *brännvin* glasses that are heavy but hold less!"

"Colditz, really!" remarks Willy.

"Yes," says Bengt, "you know of it?" Willy thinks he's going to hear a much-told story, to which the others appear resigned, after a shuffling of feet and refilling of glasses.

"*The Great Escape* movie came out while I was in high school, and there were books, of course. *Reach for the Sky*." Willy thinks, I want to hear this story. Tunnels and all sorts, even a glider. These were our heroes, mix of Brits, Dutch, Norwegians, Canadians, playing silly-enough escape games to grip us, with a grim Boche response giving it a religious tinge. Bastid Bosch, Boches, whatever it was.

"You must have been the only Swede in Colditz," says Willy.

"Joost was a Dutch air force pilot, and Frans was suspected to be a spy and a degenerate," says Adela. She has thus abridged the story, to the evident relief of all except Joost; Frans is hardly embarrassed to be called a *degenerate*, but neither of the two seems inclined to re-open the drawer she just closed. Later, seems to be promised.

"Neither of them knew Steve McQueen."

"No no, that was way before Steve McQueen," says Bengt. "You are thinking about that other one, the Great Escapade I think." Willy pulls his ear to recall actuality.

"So, how do you like Dalarna for twenty minutes at air plane speeds just above the ground?" Adela asks, effecting an escape from that muddle.

"Yes, it goes by quickly! I see what Rolf said: it is going back to forest, young forest, and a lot of summer camps."

"We produce a lot of emigrants, even still," says Bengt. "A hundred years ago they were all going to America or going in the lake, about half and half. Now they go to Saab in Göteborg or to Costa Brava."

"I am reading a book for class," says Willy, 'about tourists coming up here somewhere and telling other tourists an abandoned house foundation is a warrior's grave. They talk to a retired shoemaker, who shows them his shop and tells them a *lie* is a shaft to a scythe, an *orv*. I do not recall why. It also talks about people 'going in the lake.' Cut a hole in the ice in dead of winter and creep under it."

"But, Willy, what an indispensable thing to have learned what an *orv* is, or was! How few in this country still know that! Ja ha," says Bengt in Swedish.

"Indisp . . ."

"Indispensable, cannot get by without it!"

"When I bought it, my first book in Swedish, I asked for a dictionary to help. The very nice lady asked me to repeat it, without smiling, very politely, and wanted to know what I needed it for. Then she explained that a dictionary is a word book, whereas I had asked for a proverb."

"You see," Rolf shouts, "a dangerous person! Poor woman."

"You should have insisted on the proverb," laughs Bengt.

Rolf and Adela go off into a sidebar conversation, in suddenly some rolling dialect Willy does not follow, laundry and diet, study, furrowed brows. So Willy knocks on the door of Colditz again with Frans and Joost. Three years me and two him, yes of course we know your movies too, they were not so truthful, except that, of course, a movie is two hours or so, not years.

"Here comes Svea," observes Bengt. Willy half hears the words, then another car coming down the drive. It stops at the kitchen end of the house, and two women are glimpsed going past the lilac bush into the house.

"Rolf's sister. Ah, he did not tell you he has a sister!"

"And she is called Svea!" from Rolf. Ah so, Rolf; a bit goofy here, this *ta da*! Have you been plotting, you bugger. Flash on Rolf's heavy eyebrow thing over Dottirsmor.

"She picked up Taavi too," says Adela.

"Aha, the swan of Tuonela," says Rolf to Bengt.

"It is a neighbor, a widow," says Adela to Willy. "She said she would come for a little. She is an historian. Husband died a few years ago, and she moved out of the city to their old farmhouse across the road, lives alone."

"Tuonela, Sibelius," says Joost. "Mournful French Horn."

"Actually *cor anglais*, the swan singing to itself in the Kalevala realm of the dead," whispers Adela. "Now hush."

Fram has shambled off through the smithy between the piles, and a greeting is heard through the bark of dog and an evident kneeler and grappler, old lovers apologetic for elapsed time, ears to be rolled and snuffled, and mumbles and slobber to be exchanged. Adela and Bengt: "Taavi, so glad you came." And general exchanges, all the permutations between those familiar, and introductions for the unfamiliar.

"We have been speaking English for the benefit of Joost and Willy, and occasional Swedish for Willy to give us some comedy."

Taavi, swan of Tuonela, has white hair drawn in a bun and transparent skin. Seeing blue shadow in thin bridge of the nose, Willy thinks, at first, she looks more like a sea eagle than a swan, but what leaks from under the heavy lids is deepest dusk. Behind her comes Sis, the Svea, brushing dog hair from hands on a small towel.

Willy sees a busting through from dark to light, trailed by Fram, a black-haired and black-eyed pale young woman who stuns. The hair is cropped short. On her right face and throat, from collar bone to mid cheek, is a purple-brown blaze, a birth mark like a pennant under which she advances. She speaks with a quiet voice, a general greeting endorsed by here-she-is-dog, *awwrgh*. All have risen, embraces and introductions ensue. "Svea!" Bengt kisses her forehead when she bends to him, and they touch hairlines for the count of a loon call from the lake. Then Rolf says, "This is Willy, from my hall, from, ah, Australia."

Willy is staring and knows it. The birthmark is something between a damascene sword and an iris, regal as he apprehends it; but his gaze flutters to the others' and he catches flickers of equivocations in the greetings to Svea—she has wounded some of them in the past. But, oh! says a voice in his intestines.

Taavi, Willy wonders, should she be addressed as Doctor, Professor? But the titles are not offered; she befriends the shadows. As Taavi and Adela exchange murmurs, this Svea does the rounds, finally a glance and, in English, "So you are Rolf's friend." He takes the hand, not proffered, cool moist from wash in the house, with odd dog hairs still adhering.

"Svea is a rather regal name," Willy says. "Is Svealand not the realm of Queen Svea?"

Adela says quickly, "Not a queen. Svea is not such a rare name, but it does refer to Svealand, which was named for the old Sviar people, so *Sviars rik*."

"And, of course, your English version of the name Sweden comes from Dutch," smiles Joost. Taavi nods slightly, ambivalent agreement or let-it-pass.

"My friend Lasse was highly amused at bags of turnips on the side of the road in Tasmania, with a sign: *Swedes for sale, one dollar a bag*. He sent photos to all his old friends," recalls Willy.

"There is always fun to be found where languages overlap," says Frans, "though often it is dark humor. We call them rutabagas in Sweden and Swedes in Amsterdam, and pray, don't you Joost, 'from the wrath of the Northmen and the bitterness of Swedes, O Lord deliver us.'"

"Of course, it was a staple in Colditz, much hated, and I still cannot get over Frans trying to serve it in our house. What were you thinking?" General laughter.

"Uncle Frans has a kitchen in that house, which is itself a theater, with more knives than the royal armory. But he has been converted to the Indonesian cuisine by Joost's people, and it is sambal and coconut and fire from every bodily orifice all day long there." Rolf trembles in this mixed homage and complaint.

"Have you been in Indonesia?" Svea asks Willy. "It is surely next door to Australia."

"No."

"Just no? That is a very simple answer."

Yes, I am a simple person, a dullard. He blushes.

Taavi touches his elbow. "Truth may be simple."

"I was once in Australia," she continues. "My husband had a sabbatical year in Melbourne, and I took a study year too. I found it . . . difficult, the city. Once we flew to Alice Springs to see the interior, after seeing Sidney Nolan's *Desert Storm* paintings. You know of Nolan?"

"I recall photos. I think the actual work—big panels, no?—were still in storage then, argued over by, um, I think the city of Perth."

"Yes, I think that is so. We were writing monographs and a book about nomadic peoples—Lapps, Tuaregs, Australians. Those who said they did not own the land, the land owned them, and how they fared with the European colonists. The Australians were sensitive about a Scandinavian digging around in their history; and they were mostly happier when Nolan stayed in England."

"Yes, I bet," says Willy.

"The interior was very dramatic from the air, hot and dusty on the ground."

"It did me in," says Willy. "I got heatstroke, nearly killed me."

"Ah, so you were out there!" exclaims Taavi.

"Yes. I was a company geologist prospecting for minerals. I lived in it, roaming around, camping out, not quite a different spot every night, but not in a city more than five days a month. I was attached to it, actually. Though 'it' was a very big thing, not a campsite."

"But you left, because . . ."

"Well, the stroke caused some brain damage. I had some fuzzy bits and memory loss, and was told I should not go back in the heat, for a while, anyway. So I came to recover and find someone else to be."

"Many would be, or should be, jealous of a chance to become someone new." Taavi half-smiles.

Willy says, yes, but is a bit flustered that the slapstick answers so often repeated are failing him. "I do not feel altogether in charge of my recovery. Maybe I will turn out to be, um, a useless person, and have to give my bones to Rolf for study."

Rolf sees Willy is sagging, and says, a nudge, "Willy has his own story about the blacks of Australia."

Willy takes a deep breath, they are waiting for him to deliver, so then, "When I got heatstroke, we had just found a grave marker with a metal sign saying 'P Mack, killed by blacks, 1894.' He was a prospector like me, except I was a company man with a Land Rover. When the sun went down, a full moon came up, and the flies kept crawling, and the temperature stayed over forty Celsius all night. It was sort of my, my, oh well." He is intimidated by the gaze of Taavi and disoriented by the mirror ball of Svea. Bugger it, then. Give them P Mack:

> "Way back then,
> All a these jokers was roamin' in the bush . . . "

He has to wipe his eyes when he is done, feeling unaccountably emotional. Crikey. Damned eyes letting down all the time, I should have asked someone about that, is it drug or fuzzies.

"Thank you for that," says Taavi with the wanest smile. "But, of course, not so long ago; I was alive then."

Joost says wickedly, "Willy goes from blush to blush."

Rolf to the rescue. "Willy could always start a restaurant. He does this peanut butter chicken. Have you heard of such a thing? We have these parties in the hall, more and more people come."

"Of course we have peanut sauces, which go with many satay foods. What is yours like, Willy?" asks Frans.

"Ah, mine is quite simple, like me, but sometimes flops."

"Whereas Frans's is complicated and always succeeds, so far as we know, since he keeps us out of his kitchen," from Joost.

"Tell them, Willy, how yours is the 'proletarian' sauce'," says Rolf, egging on the competition.

"Ah, well, firstly you must use the cheap peanut butter, as Rolf says, with the little bit of sugar which you carefully allow to caramelize it, then cayenne and basil, then swooshes of peanut oil and sherry to get the right thickness."

"Maybe we can have a cook-off tomorrow!" says Bengt to Adela. "If I get a list I can go to town."
"Willy's PBC parties got so popular now some Norrlanders on the north hall want to do a sour herring party next week, damn!"

"Now, there is a clash of civilizations! Or, at any rate, of a culture with any civilization in the same weather system! Have you heard about this sour herring, Willy? It is partially fermented in brine and still fermenting in the can, which bulges at the ends. If you open a can in Uppsala, the Norrland students will go upwind to find it, just to get drunk, and everyone else will shut their windows and call the fire department." Bengt is amused to educate Willy in national idiosyncracies.

"Sounds exciting! Which way would each of you go?"

Taavi shudders, but says she used to like it when she was young. Seems to be general agreement amongst the rest that none of them is quite northern enough to exactly relish the experience of sour herring, but Rolf is looking forward to the party as spectacle. He especially is amused to think of observing Willy there, as were the prospective hosts from across the hall. Not even the Norrland student nation is willing to host a sour herring event in their Uppsala building, but there is the wooded area next to the Flogsta block, where Willy works out, and which has, apparently, ample buffers to "get away with it, at least at first." Norrlands Nation has offered assistance, should the hosts want it, and it is not clear how many the "help" would be. All but Joost and Willy here in Dalarna appear to have been exposed to this totemic stuff, and Joost is less curious than appalled at the rumors.

"So, Willy, why are you here rather than London?" from Svea as others discuss international positions on sour herring, whether it contravenes treaty law, etc. She has been watching him coolly. When he meets her gaze he sees she is assessing whether he is as odd as his un-Swedish clothes, and whether he will flinch before her blaze.

"Yes, the British colonials still think that London is the center of the empire and go to Soho like pilgrims. Not me. I had a Swede working with us some time ago, and I thought, Well why not try that?"

Svea looks upon him plainly wondering if he is a simpleton, or pretending to be one, or what. He looks upon Svea and feels as if something has been slipped in his drink.

"I do not understand the mosquitoes; I thought there should be many more," Willy breaks out to Adela. "I read of moose standing on the side of the road to take the breeze of a passing car, or running to death."

"Well, it is late in the bug season," says Adela, "but Svea is our mosquito expert."

"Ah, but ours are too boring for Svea. She only likes the tropical ones with diseases. Actually, it is that parasite she is in love with," says Bengt.

Svea tucks her chin as if loath to get into a lecture, but there it is, all are looking at her.

To Willy, "There are not so many this year." A deep breath.

"In some bad years they have sprayed, but there is a wide distrust of pesticides. The Rachel Carson DDT thing. And the larvae, which are what the pesticides attack, are part of the ecology. They feed the water fowl and small fish that feed the big fish.

"And then some of the Dalarna folk like to say to the tourists, *what mosquitoes*? Like Far. There are even some who will crush them on their skin and eat them, saying this makes them—what is it?—repellent. Mostly it is psychology. If you must live with them, you do; and if you move to Stockholm, you cannot come back in a bad year. If Far and Frans each put a hand in a box of Dalarna mosquitoes, they will get bitten about the same, depending on how many Indonesian peppers each has eaten the day before.

"They do not carry diseases in Scandinavia now, but there was a malaria problem once, all the way up to the Arctic Circle. Between about 1800 and 1880, did you know that Far? Malaria would break out in the spring, even though the air temperature never reached what we thought was the minimum for the Plasmodium protozoan which causes malaria. Of course, we have many Anopheles mosquito species, all the way to Murmansk, but the Plasmodium needs the warmth. So it seems the mosquito females copulated in the summer and semi-hibernated in winter indoors, in stables and big rooms where people huddled for warmth, and took blood meals and cross-infected people of all ages and animals, and laid their eggs in the spring."

Again to Willy, "You know that only the females bite people? Males and females get most nutrition from plants, nectar, but the female needs protein to develop the eggs.

"My research subject has been one species that gets its protein from other mosquito larvae, but is otherwise vegetarian. Obviously you cannot ask those ones to eat up all the people-biters, but we are trying to find how much they can attenuate the problems in the tropics."

Willy is agog. He looks to the others just to not stare at this young woman, Rolf's sister, and be seen by all to be staring. But nobody else says anything immediately, so he asks, "How long have mosquitoes been around?"

"At least as long as birds, I think. They probably fed on the dinosaurs, and certainly the first mammals. We do not know how old is the symbiosis of Anopheles and Plasmodium. But there are other mosquito species and other parasites, bacterial and viral, so yellow fever and dengue."

"But, birds! Jurassic then!"

"Yes, but that is the mosquito. You are a geologist, yes. I do not know how old the malaria Plasmodium is. There are, of course, many Plasmodium types as well. It is interesting that they have chloroplasts, so they may have evolved from algae, perhaps along with mosquitoes, possibly much later."

Adela says, "Svea, you sound as if you had just given a lecture! No no, I mean it is nice to hear you speak as a professional to your dreary family."

"Yes," says Taavi, and bequeaths a tiny benevolent smile. A few million mosquito enounters in her life.

In accepting another *brännvin* pour from Frans, Willy has come to Svea's side. He does not have to look at her now. She smells of . .

. what? It is familiar. Damn, it' s the same damned bitters soap he has. Or is it just that he is effusing it in a sweat here?

"Bitters soap," whispers Willy, just loud enough for her to hear. Hears her breathe. They are side by side, addressing each other through the bottle on the table. He feels odd, an aura coming on? Observing himself, like a chess pawn shuttled up, withdrawn, stared through by the other players, crikey. Edge of dread. Not the aura, but he is not, well, in himself altogether, at least what he thinks is himself. Brush her hand then: both jump as if startled at a static spark.

Svea regards him with—what is it, scorn? Although, perhaps she is just looking across her nose with weapon cocked on the other side of her face. "The soap is in the toilet, of course." He sees that she is quizzical at his demeanor, and he wonders if he is in fact falling in a "fuzzy bit".

Joost remarks, seeming oblivious to the atmosphere, "So, Svea, what is this new angle in school? I understand emergency medical, and, what is it, French?"

Svea takes half a step away from Willy and quietly says, "There are limited research funds in tropical diseases when there are no epidemics. This could put me in a medical relief program where an epidemic started."

"And French because the international medical programs are still French," says Frans.

"*Oui, précis.*"

"Damn," says Rolf. "I am glad French is not a requirement for me. If a Frenchman complained to me of a broken toe, I would stick an airway down his throat for his respiratory problem."

"At least," says Joost, "the medical relief programs are not all stolen by the rulers of those third world countries. We saw donated clothing being sold in Angola in makeshift stalls, right out of the UNESCO crates." *Angola*, thinks Willy, what bell does that ring?

"Actually," murmurs Taavi, "the aid and even the medical teams are often co-opted by the local militia, where there is conflict, to serve their own soldiers. In Africa or Indochina."

"Svea," says Adela.

"Mother is saying, in code, it is escapism on my part, but misguided because it is dangerous," says Svea. Bengt, who is edging by to go pee, squeezes his daughter's shoulder. She tenses, then briefly touches his hand as he goes by. Lots of family code here.

Svea says to him, "So, Willy, you are making a social experiment, playing Myshkin the Idiot, you know Dostoyevsky? Until some rich woman picks you up to look after her Baltic island copper mine and her dogs, is it?"

"Svea!" says her mother.

Willy: "Uh." Meaning, he is in disarray.

Franz manages to get in a question to Svea. "We have not seen you in some time, not since your Vienna trip. How did that go?"

"So-so. Malaria is not so fashionable with the WHO trumpeting the end of smallpox in the near future. We did see Aida at the opera, but also suffered a stuffy Offenbach and Strauss concert."

"We? Did you go with your Professor, Wenz is it?"

Willy notes that Svea gives no answer but for an icy glare. "I hate waltzes," he says. Then immediately feels the stupid klutz.

Svea turns to him. "So you cannot appreciate the pinnacle of nineteenth century European civilization that is the Viennese waltz?"

But Willy sees a glint in her eye. Rolf says, "When you were here at my Gymnasium graduation, you, sister mine, went on about waltzes as emblematic of Euro-fascism!"

All breathe in and turn to the conversation Joost has been having with Bengt about restoration of old wrought iron in Amsterdam street facades. "There is a lot of work there, mostly Germans are coming in, they have some big shops."

"So, Willy," intervenes Adela, "you probably have a family somewhere that misses you?"

Willy struggles. Let's not be glib now, he thinks, because somehow things are different here, today.

"There are, of course, parents and siblings, two, and uncountable cousins. A dairy farm with a hundred or so cows and eighty pigs, in fences and pens. At five thirty in the morning and three thirty in the afternoon, the cows all walk down the trails to the milking shed, except those that have just dropped calves, who get to stay in the paddock with their young for a few days, until they are separated. The male calves are put out in a pen for collection by the vealer truck . . . We all leave in trucks or buses, but mostly do not go far, few cross the Great Waters as the I Ching has it . . . I am sorry, I cannot say all of this in Swedish, I have never tried it. It is all like the broken down old hay baler in the overgrown iron shed—not exactly forgotten, but pretty much abandoned."

Adela says, "Our cities are full of farm boys, from your age up. And many 'crossed the great waters,' as you say. Some younger sons still cling fiercely to family farms here, and I find they are quite competitive in their fatalism about the future of those farms."

"But most of our farmers who left went to America to start new farms there fifty or a hundred years ago," says Taavi. "Do you know the *Emigrants* series by Moberg?"

"Only in translation. So far, the first," says Willy.

"But there were many more farmers gone to America, as in the *Emigrants*, than gold-seeking Macks, and more farmers' children writing about them than anyone about Macks," says Frans. "And history depends on who writes it, no?" he directs to Taavi.

"It is no secret that my perspective, and Holger's—Holger was my husband—is not mainstream. We explored the histories of minorities," says Taavi to Willy. "In Australia, we got into difficulties over attempts to investigate the government kidnapping of so-called 'half-caste' aboriginal children, for instance, and putting them in missions or adopting them out. And the Kola Lapps did not experience the same nineteenth century as the Muscovites who colonized the peninsula, they became serfs."

"Ech," says Frans. "I didn't mean to challenge you, Taavi, we are, I think, all aware of your efforts to right the wrongs—heroic, even. I wish I had thought to bring my copy of your book, to ask you to sign it."

"Which book?" asks Taavi. Actually, there has been only the one published; it is a mischievous question. Without waiting for Frans to dig up an answer, she touches Bengt on the elbow, and says, "Bengt is the real antiquarian amongst us."

"No, no," says Bengt, "I have made some railings for a couple of museums, but I also make things that are needed by individuals, one-off items, not just for farmhouses and cemeteries."

Taavi laughs. "I like to tease Bengt about these things, when he is not hammering away."

"So," says Adela, standing to top up *brännvin* glasses all round, "Willy and Svea must declare life plans, while the old-timers can just swim around in histories with *brännvin*."

General laughter. Frans tips his glass to Rolf: "While Rolf, the doctor-priest, watches over us and our medicines. Have you got past revulsion at the dissection of the bodies of the indigent yet,

Rolf?"

"Usch," utters Rolf. Lab experiences have been a crypt he has not been able to talk about much. He would have liked to talk about it with Willy on the way up, but for the racket of the decrepit muffler. He was leery of the almost-intimacy of brief sharing of feelings with one or another fellow student. He shudders now, recalling sharing a cadaver in anatomy class, nothing in common past sharing the tracing of the urethra of a corpse, but astounding to each of them at the time.

"Priest!" says Svea to Rolf. "What do you think of that?"

Svea squeezes his arm. Willy sees the relationship between them has been adversarial for much of their lives, pierced by tentative affections such as this now. What solvent, he wonders.

"Fra Rolf, Far Bengt, stitchers of torn flesh, old bridges and tortured iron," she murmurs, and tips a toast, "*Skål!*"

"And you, dear sister," gives Frans to Adela. "Your birthday, again, and our father's, which art in heaven!"

"He means, our father the atheist pastor, whose birthday is tomorrow," says Adela to Willy, "and who had a Bible signed by Selma Lagerlöf, the author, because it was the only paper at hand he could have her autograph!" Joost titters at these northern folk tipping, tipsying. The said Bible has a place in Frans's office, on an end of a shelf with mementoes, just because of that signature.

"Did you not know Lagerlöf also, Taavi?" asks Bengt, who knows, of course, she did.

"A little, from the university," says Taavi. "Adela, I should be going soon to let the dog out. I could borrow your bicycle." Adela insists, however, it is dark now. Well, Taavi will use the restroom first. Willy steps into the shop to allow her to pass, and she pauses there to speak to him.

"It seems unlikely you can go back."

"Back? I cannot face that wicked heat, yet anyway. And the future is forward, not back."

"But what about that other, the farm, where you grew up?"

"Ah, humility nuzzling the flanks of cows and washing the udders for the cups. Made me vegetarian for a while. Where, then, were you born?"

"In Russian Finland. I spent much of my life learning the history of others before I could penetrate the history of my own childhood."

Willy looks at his feet as she slips past, suddenly conscious of how little he knows compared to this woman who is, what, three times his age but who has captured a vein, at least, of centuries of intelligence, which dwarfs his own mineral show of knowledge, particularly his apprehension of humanity—what the hell we mean, collectively.

When she comes back out, he says, "Actually, I think I have lost the sense of history, sort of. I mean the relational contexts." And she sees he has been stuck in that thought all the while she was gone.

"Well, your adventures in language are, of course, disorienting. I would say, enjoy the comedy while you can, don't be disappointed when the new becomes old, as it does by the minute."

"It is funny," Willy responds, "I was just speaking with a Polish guy in our apartments, and agreeing with him, I think, that the difficulty of communicating in a language neither of us is any good at makes us think too hard what we are trying to say, so it is both very sincere and likely to collapse into silliness. We amuse the Swedes, but we struggle with one another, and it is painful but humorous to drink a beer together, the two of us."

"Willy, you should not be a tourist in your own life. You should find some therapist help. Oh, you will be all right. Be careful with that Svea. She could drown you if you do not keep a grip."

"What?"

"Yes, I see a boy eying a trembling horse eying him, that will bolt, with him aboard, into the lake."

Taavi goes on through to the house, leaving Willy palpitating in the shadow. He drifts out of the corner and back into the group.

"Aha, we thought Taavi had run off with you," says Adela in a soft voice.

"Willy, you are so serious suddenly. Did Taavi intimidate you?" Rolf jokes.

"Yes, she did. That is to say . . . I mean, she asked me to check on you when you have to do anatomy labs." Guffaws from the Dutch contingent, sighs from Bengt and Adela, who recognize it as a jest but feel sometimes anxious about the actual sensitivity alluded to in their son, the earnest one.

Adela is just getting up to take Taavi home, when Taavi comes back down the passage. She bids everyone goodnight, and the two go out together. Taavi says in passing to Willy, "A student of mine from some years ago now lives in the Waitakere Range, and sounds as if he wants to live out his days there, one of the few crossing the equator in that direction. His Swedish is fading. I think he writes occasionally to exercise it, but partly to show he has passed into a new person, although he cannot really say who he is."

Wave, and gone. Leaving a speechless vortex.

Then there are just Svea and the guys.

A phone rings, and Bengt pouts in the direction of the noise, and then gets up and walks around a corner. After a few staccato hejs and hellos he comes back in and says to Frans and Joost, "It is for you, I think." Joost goes to take it, and Frans says, "That will be Anna, Joost's niece."

Bengt sits back down. "That is the one who . . ."

"Yes." To the others, Frans relates that Anna recently arrived from Java with her three kids and they are staying with them while she tries to sort out compensation from Dutch or Indonesian governments, and her husband, the father. The family plantation was confiscated by Suharto; the husband was a derelict who had "gone native".

"We thought briefly about bringing them here, but infants you know. In the first couple of days they were interesting, then exhausting, but now Joost is attached to them, and I cannot easily confess it but I too will be happy and sad to see them go. The boy plays a fair game of chess, learning fast even as I fade."

"Children would be . . ," begins Rolf, and thinks better of it.

"How old are they?" asks Willy.

"About one, three and six," muses Frans.

"Tell Joost to ask her how many jet engines on her plane!" Willy's request startles the others, who look upon him with variously wide eyes, frowns; what now?

Frans nonetheless goes off and is heard to speak with Joost. He is soon back. "He did not understand; she did not understand; well, I do not understand."

Joost has sat down again, giving Willy an odd look, when the phone rings again. Bengt says, "That will be for you, nobody calls me at this hour." So Joost goes back to the phone, and there is a volley of short Dutch questions and incredulities. He returns and, standing in front of Willy, says, "The boy said there were five jets!"

"Bloody hell!"

"And she asked, is it the kidnapper. But she would not say more."
All are looking at him intently, breathing held. Willy stares at Rolf,
yes Rolf, this is me, no I am not flipping out.

So he goes into an explanation, crowd in the hangar, his holding the
girl when they were obliged to shuffle in disorderly throng through
ticket stomping chutes and out to the jumbo jet, the separation
and panic; and then the spare engine strapped to one wing, not
seen until sunrise, the purser in five languages, "And that is how
we do it!"

When he is done there is an awful tension, finally broken by Joost.
"Well that is too much."

Svea blurts, "That is just too improbable Willy. The Norns have
been sporting with you, and it feels perilous to stand too close to
you!"

"Well, it is certainly improbable, but not any more momentous
than finding a sock behind the drier!"

"I think you should go to Amsterdam with Frans and Joost, and see
if she, this Anna, wants to kill you or marry you, and then send us a
lost or found postcard!"

Frans and Joost look queryingly upon one another, and after some
muttering and waggling of shoulders and hands, Joost goes off into
the house to call back, leaving a sputtering group, unbelievable!
oh my!

Frans proffers more *brännvin* all round, and a chuckle or two
promise the tension is dissipating. He pours a glass for Willy and
hands it to Svea to pass to him. Svea has picked up a feather off the
deck, long and black with flashes of blue green, and twirls it in her
left hand. Svea extends the glass and the feather in two hands. She
declines another glass herself. The improbability of Willy and his

adventures have loosened her defenses and thinks she should not drink any more. Willy extends his right hand to take the glass from her right, pauses, not sure if the feather is also offered, holds his left hand out. Awkward moment. She looks him in the eye, gives him the feather, and says, "*Skata.*"

Willy does not know this word and wonders, and Frans rescues him, "Magpie."

"Ah. *Skata*, you say." The magpie is a most royal bird, dwells in a diamond tree. "You know, your *skata*, is it, is very different from the Australian magpie. This one is very royally colored, and graceful. The Australian magpie, I do not think it is even related. It is black and white, flies like a clown, and sings oodle ardle awdle. That, and Waltzing Matilda, are the real national anthems. And the kookaburra call."

Svea is still standing with two hands extended, herself a bit confused by this translation of birds. "So, you would say your birds are more democratic and better singers than ours?"

"I would not say one is better, and I would not say any of them are yours or mine." He hands the feather back to her; too, heavy?

"What is the cuckoo thing?"

"A kookaburra is a big kingfisher with a very loud, laughing call. You hear it on Australian movie reels. I cannot do it justice, but something like *kookuckookarklekorkelkoo*." Rising to a choking gargle, he finishes in awkwardness.

"Jaha."

He is embarrassed but he has her eye; he sees she is stuck as he is. So, he reaches out to give the feather again, and she takes it, and blinks. Frans, Joost, and Bengt are as nonplussed as she is at this handing back and forth, and Rolf scratches his head. "Are you sure it's not the crow?"

"One cannot be sure of anything tonight," says Svea.

***

Taavi says to Adela, "Svea has changed. I mean, not just the hair. Her lovely hair, I wondered why she cut it."

"Yes. She has become even more introverted, perhaps depressed sometimes, with only spells of the old sarcasm. How she was flirting with that boy! Only I doubt he was clever enough to notice."

"Oh, he noticed! They were on different wavelengths, like cello and timpani, but they were playing to each other. Perhaps a brief flirtation."

"Of course, one is not surprised Svea would be fascinated by a boy who is not the epitome of Swedish tradition. I wonder how innocent Rolf was in orchestrating this. They elude us, these children."

"Bengt said he likes them better since he has given up trying to understand them."

"Well. Taavi, I have not told Bengt this. There was an affair of perhaps a year, with a prof in her department, Wenz. Which ended awkwardly since they still had to work together. Actually, Bengt knows that. What he doesn't know is . . . well, an abortion."

"Ah. Adela, my dear friend, Bengt told me much the same thing, in fact, though he only suspected the . . You should take a turn around the lake to talk about this. He doesn't know what it is precisely, but it is not sitting well with him, not voicing it."

"Taavi, I could be jealous of you with my husband, that you talk so easily together."

"Of course I am older than his dead mother. We do not talk easily but carefully, which is one of the reasons it is precious. You know I cringe to think of his awful shop coffee with the metal taste, but when one drinks it, one gets used to it, and I am ashamed to offer him my good coffee when he brings the mail."

"He always says he is privileged to talk with you, as if you were a visiting dignitary rather than a friend and neighbor."

"I have to go to Stockholm next week. Are you free one evening? We could have a proper talk."

"Yes. You have my office phone number? Call me. They will send a car for you, yes? Thank you for coming. Good night."

Taavi thinks, poor Adela is more afflicted by that daughter than Svea is by her stain. That Svea is still certainly unconventional, at once cruel, introverted. I would not wish a traditional marriage on her any more than I wanted one myself, but . . . It feels as if she and that boy clashed and were shockingly not incompatible. Willy's principal strength seems to be what they call his idiocy. A child prince with a few missing parts. Myshkin indeed, Dostoyevsky's epileptic saint. And stricken!

***

"It is just a two-minute drive," Rolf tells Willy; but the way Rolf drives that could be a ways. Bengt says to Rolf that her—Taavi's—cataracts have become worse. She cannot drive anymore, and she is contemplating doing the surgery.

"Do you know her book?" asks Willy. "What language would it be in?"

"Oh, I do not have it, though I should," says Bengt. "I am sure it is in Swedish or German." Bengt and Frans exchange quips about Taavi's work which Willy cannot follow.

Bengt says to Svea, "I had better hold the evening meal for a bit. Those two will have to chat about all of us."

"We are not so important. They will talk briefly about Taavi's memoirs and Mor's hospital reorganization, and she will be back in ten minutes."

Frans says, "So, we should talk about the children, if they will not. We have not seen you for three years, I think. Rolf, we were worried about you being the boy from the country but not a country boy, how you would fare in the world, priest or doctor. I am relieved to see it is the doctor. And Svea, fairy child, emerging from the lake to take on all the mosquito races!"
"Uncle, we do not live in the fairy stories of our father's mother."

"Yes, she was a character," says Bengt. To Willy and Joost he explains, "My mother thought life a drama where things, even seasons, changed by the breaking and making of spells. She said Svea was a *näck's* child, a *näck* being a water spirit that sings to seduce women and children and lure them away, maybe to drown them. They seem to have mostly emigrated, too, the old fairy folk."

Willy says to Svea, and tenses up as he utters, "*Es tu vraiment une Lorelei?*" Jesus, what did I say?

Svea tilts her head at him and flutters a mocking look. "*Français de sous-terre. Je suis ce que je suis.*"

Willy thinks, ha! I recognize that. "*Je suis pas ce que je suis.*"

Amusement competing with disdain, she continues, "*Si je suis ce que je suis . . .*"

"*Alors, je suis pas ce que je suis!*"

"*Personne qui suivait l'ane,*" explains Svea to Frans, who has cocked his ear quizically. "Man following the ass."

"Ah," he says, "forgot all I ever knew."

"You tell it," she says.

"I am what I am, not what I follow; if I am what I follow then I am not what I am. Wow, that is at least ten years buried. You know, not one person in this country has understood a word of the schoolboy French I tried."

"Oh, isn't that strange," she mocks. "Perhaps you should stay with Australian, and then it would not matter."

"*Je ne suis pas Australien vraiment.*"

"No, but it follows you all the same, like your ass." And she moves past, to the toilet.

"Well, Australia. You might have heard," Willy says to Joost, the one-time Dutch Air Force pilot, "there was a guy, a geologist, in Hobart who solved a paratroopers' problem in the war, I mean your last. Many parachutes were not opening, so they were going splat, and he theorized it was because the cords were twisted as they were packed, but that they could be readily untwisted by flailing one arm in big circles while the trooper was falling. And he demonstrated this himself by deliberately twisting a chute's cords and jumping with it. He was a prof famous for promoting continental drift, then going off on the wrong tangent. I went into the geology department to get him to sign a copy of his book for me. Another slightly crazy hero."

Where was I going with that, he wonders? Perhaps just dodging out.

"Joost was the pilot," says Frans. "Did you hear of that, Joost?"

"No, but I was captured early. At the beginning, the parachute was like a first aid kit—a joke."

"I wish I had thought to bring up his name when Taavi was here. He was also a pioneer in New Guinea, a solitary white amongst the Sepik tribes," says Willy.

"So, Willy," observes Svea coming back in to the gathering, "that should have been your destiny, perhaps? They were headhunters, no, these Sepik?" Svea cocks her head at him.

"With lots of mosquitoes. Perhaps they would have been happy hunting for you, Svea. I cannot say what I should have done, ever. I followed yellow brick roads to a cliff and fell over it."

"Were you looking for a brain, or just trying to get home to Kansas?"

"Look, I'm not so interesting as everyone else here, and I have lost track of even the path I was on. Let me just listen, rather than be the wasp on the fruit."

"Ja, Svea, do not pick on my friend; he feeds me sometimes," interjects Rolf.

Bengt waves a hand. "But Willy, the wasp on the fruit, as you say, you are a bit fascinating to us provincials. Maybe Frans and Joost can compare the foundations of Venice and the new towns on the polders and the food in Colditz and Amsterdam, but to me and my needling daughter, you are indeed the buzz." A bit of a wicked look at that Svea from both Bengt and Rolf.

A citronella candle gutters. Svea shuffles and says, "I will go to the house and get candles."

Bengt does not say, there are candles here, because Willy has pushed off, "I will go with you."

Conversation drops behind them as he follows her out. Breaths are held. She does not say, she hardly needs help. She is thinking, this weird person pushing at my door, if not ugly beyond words then at least so un-Swedish, what in hell? Willy is thinking, this is not a *fuzzy bit*, is it, not the usual signs, but, shit, I am stricken, what in hell? As they go up the gravel in the fading light, he asks, "Can you see?" She, in a guttural whisper, "I do not need." "Yes!" In the entry, she reaches into a high cabinet, takes out one candle, turns, and gives it to him, shoulders brushing, and turns back for another. There. As they go out, she asks, dripping sarcasm, "Can you manage?"

"We shall see, we shall see!"

The onsetting evening chill seems heavy with stifled voices. Each glances at the other and away, and down. Willy feels like Punch in the puppet show expecting the rolling pin: hit me now! Sounds and scents of the forest pulse, and the path plays jokes with his footsteps.

When they reach the others again, the candles are both lit ceremoniously in grave silence. Glances are diplomatic, suspenseful. Bengt asks bravely, "So, Willy, you will perhaps be needing another sup?"

"Sir," says Willy. And then, "Really, I did not need that one five glasses before. I was, of course, only trying to, ah, honor your hospitality, and the minor concern that I would make a fool of myself, well. I am honored to be foolish in your company. I mean, oh hell."

"I understand, I think. Listen, I am glad you have come to us, I thank Rolf for that, you have been very entertaining and I hope you enjoy the weekend here. Oops, my glass is also empty. I must have tipped it over."

Svea says, "Several wasps here drunk on fermenting fruit."

"Please. I am, of course, a little drunk. And sentimentally so. On top of being an idiot. But all of you, and Taavi and Adela, and this lake in a dale. And this smithy with the smell of beaten iron. If . . . Well, I am deeply moved in all my parts."

"Willy, you should stand for election, or take a glass of water and an aspirin."

"Yes, I am sorry to be so noisy, asking you to let me shut up and listen."

"No," says Svea, "go on. I am interested to see you self-destruct."

"Very well. Yes. Self-destruct."

Willy carefully pushes his chair back and kneels on the floor, at first unsteadily. Now then! All sit up, stop breathing.

"Herr Bengt, Sir."

"Willy!"

"I feel I have arrived at the place that . . . I mean . . . It feels the most important thing in my life is to make a complete fool of myself right now, that nothing else ever has or will matter as much as this moment. Damn! So I . . . Well then . . . I beg permission to be taken on as your apprentice; and also, I beg permission to be your son-in-law."

Even Fram is silent, rumbling breath held.

"And, of course, your esteemed wife's—permission, that is—I will ask when . . . Well, when. As to this Svea, your daughter, her part, I understand this may be, well, less than easy, but I, too, am strong-willed."

***

"What happened?"

"It's okay. More or less."

Bengt turns out the light so he can flounder out of his clothes in the dark and cover his weary clumsiness and shut down a potentially long examination. But he realizes that is futile, and, in fact, he wants to hand off the, what, the drama. His ears are ringing.

"So."

Adela pulls pillows behind her.

"Rolf's Willy just got on his knees, I mean literally, two knees, and asked to be my apprentice and my son-in-law."

"Pshhhh!"

"Yes."

"So, he was completely drunk?"

"I would say no. He drank as much as the Hollanders, which was a lot. Rolf drank much less, but will be hungover. Svea held a glass the whole time, but I noticed her dumping it in the quench barrel. So, all drunk and a bit loud, but they sounded, well, coherent, if not sober."

"And you said?"

"I said I cannot afford an apprentice."

"And Svea screeched and ran out of there."

"Just so."

"And the others?"

"They all looked for their false teeth on the floor."

"Christ, man. How did it come to that?"

"There was, of course, a weird flirtation, deepening sarcasm on her part and the blushing idiot on his. One would say she repulsed him, but he got under her skin. Another would say the drama will have collapsed in the morning and they will not look at each other. The princess and the gypsy will rush off, each on their own way, with aspirin."

"You think that? You have a father's confidence you understand your daughter, without much foundation. And, of course, you yourself led that slalom through the bottles."

"Yes, it is all wrong. I think this Willy has rattled the shingles of this house."

"So, now you are just going to sleep?"

"Perhaps I can. Are you thinking of going to Svea? I would stay away from that maelstrom for now."

"Mmmmmm. I might as well get up and make coffee soon for anyone who wants it, the sky is lightening already. Is there anything else?"

"I don't remember anything else."

"On the first day they met! Damn! Do they not either of them recognize the other is crazy?"

"Romeo and Juliet, wife of mine."

"And how does your son esteem this barbarian he has brought to this house?"

"Rolf is quite drunk and bemused. I think he finds this fellow fascinating because he does not understand him, in several ways."

"And you?"

"Well, he is not a total lunatic at any rate, at least, hmmm. Well, we shall see in the morning if they have locked horns or if it is just crash and flight. But I fear it is the latter, I mean the former. Damn, now I will not sleep. We might as well get up and do that coffee."

"House coffee, not your shop coffee. I had a long week and was tired, but then I came up because I could not stand to see her fall from her tower."

"Again."

"Yes."

"You did not fall from a tower at her age."

"No, like an idiot I crawled and climbed into one."

"Hmnnnn."

"But . . ."

"But?"

"Two such afflicted melancholics, they will dig a hole."

"Yes but perhaps not for long."

Adela gets up on her elbow, thinks better of it, lies back and says, "Perhaps we should go to Amsterdam and let Frans cook for us for a week."

"What? Where did that come from?"

***

Rolf snores even before he is horizontal in the boathouse, but sits up suddenly and snorts and laughs, giddiness, nausea, and incredulity competing for his nasal passages, then subsides and is out. Willy lies on his back, turns to his side to escape the giddiness, too, sees recriminations in the lines of objects at floor level, and rolls onto his back again. This is not to be a simple escape into sleep, and sleep, anyway, feels more threatening than desired haven. He strains to decipher the structure of the rafters in the dark. Hold on, do not revisit the night's proceedings, too, too . . . That girl is up his nostrils, in his knuckles, but he cannot see her face. He shuts her out, and the reenactment of his drama, but he can neither escape nor hold to any of it. That Taavi, then. I should have told her about Carey, perhaps they met. I cannot remember meeting him, though he signed my book, but I remember *about* him. Bugger, a hole in the memory with sharp edges. Somewhere I read, or heard, about his Papua history, oil geologist on foot and in canoes, the only white in a jungle of warring tribes, surveyor, doctor, and trader, treating natives with parasites, malaria, typhoid, spear wounds, out of a captain's medical guide. *Not* killed by blacks. Malaria, aah; keep moving. Took up the heresy of Wegener and made it his own, evolving to the expanding earth, the book written with high derision for continental drift disbelievers, taking on the sea floor spreading shown by the magnetic polarity stripes as proof of his own thing, then stranded as the geology world lurched past into the new plate tectonics creed. I do recall " . . . every aspiring author must jump the bandwagon to gild another anther of this fashionable lily." Memorable, if not exactly measured for a science book. Painted into a corner. Why can I not remember him in person? I went to his department in Hobart; they said come back tomorrow. That I remember, and I did. Who told me—was it him?—about making theodolite crosshairs from spider web in Sepik, because the fungi? Malaria, indeed. I am undone by her, I suppose! What does that mean? Pain for certain. She will flee. Flew. Flow. Oooh. I left a wreckage, yes. Do not dwell there now, let the humiliation wait its turn. Is the dark lifting already, is it the alcohol paying a social call on the open doors of the broken synapses? Come in. No invitations necessary if you are crazy enough. I yam I yam. Iam quatit ungula campum. Drum me to sleep you ungulate mumbles. Shit, pissed as a newt.

***

At dawn, Rolf gets up to pee, stumbles across Willy and wakes him.

"Time to...?"

"Piss."

"Me too." Though Willy did not drink the half gallon of water like Rolf to try to avert a hangover, he staggers after him to the edge of the lake, and they pee into the reeds, a duet of tinkle and jangle.

"Let's see if I can find some fishing things." Rolf bangs about the boatshed and calls Willy to come help haul a battered aluminum canoe out. Willy obliges as Rolf mutters instructions and orchestrates maneuvers, invasion of the piscine kingdom while the enemy is still asleep, wooden paddles banging on canoe loud enough to wake some of whatever critters are dead in the vicinity, let alone the living, like Fram, who forlornly walks out on the dock. Rolf produces, with a flourish, a can of dirt with, what, worms, or is it perhaps anatomy class leftovers? Ugh. Despite Willy's wobblies, they are on the lake in no time it seems, with a couple of wake-up beers hanging in the water in, what are they, socks? Fram watches from the dock.

Rolf propels them with apparently casual stroking to a spot off a reedy point, where he says there is a channel on the other side, and they flip out baited hooks with floats, pop open the barely cooled beers, and settle as the ripples die to painted stillness of reflected forest and one evanescent cloudlet. There is a faint buzz of insects over a shrubby mire with brown, rainbow, manganese film at a creek inlet, but Willy cannot see an outlet, or whether there is actually a bend in the lake.

Quite quickly, Willy gets a bite, which Rolf instructs him to handle gently, then pulls up a small roach. Rolf takes the fish in gloved hand, frees the hook, and turns it back into the water. Aah. Out and back.

"Barbless."

"Yes. Best if you think you will get small ones and turn them back. You did well. So, you have done this before. Yes, you did say that."

"Once I had a friend . . . "

"Hard to imagine, but!"

"He taught me to fly fish in Tasmania."

"Yes! I remember your telling it now."

"One day, he said, 'Try dropping it on the eddy line of that big rock,' and I did, and I picked it up just right when the fish took it. A big bugger, it hunkered down in the eddy, then flared, a brown, and ran across the current to the next eddy, pulled and carried on, played dead, then ran all over the stream, threatening to take me home to meet his bloody mother. His, I say, jaw like a salmon, and all the while my friend behind me, laughing and hooting like a maniac. Finally I got that trout into deep slow water next to me, where he hid under a rock, gathering his wits. I pulled a bit harder, rod bent like a horseshoe, to pull him out of there. He came up, finally, to the surface, lay half on his side and looked me in the eye. Then he writhed and spat the barbless nymph at me and was gone. The fly hit me in the forehead and hooked me at least as well as it had him. Jock was still chuckling when he took it out.

"That fish. Saying, I guess, *take it back*, or something. I have not thought of that for a long time. Now, it seems to me it was a giving me a premonition of the thing, the thing I have, that it was born before the heatstroke."

"You mean you think, today, that you might have had the condition, whatever it is, before the stroke."

"Yes, perhaps. But it is likely just retrospective bullshit."

Rolf begins to say, That is important, but he gets a more substantial bite and winches a fifteen-inch fish into the boat. "*Gädda*. Pike. Pretty pattern." Rolf raps the fish on the head with a bleached stick on a string, and Willy sees that this whole activity is long-rehearsed, the rapping stick a venerable artifact, so that the speedy assemblage of equipment was automatic.

"If we get enough of them this size we can make a meal of them; otherwise Far will have it for dinner alone one day."

"Rolf."

"Yes, I know you want to talk about her."

"Whoa!"

"Okay. She smokes, you know. Not so often, but those self-made things with papers and loose tobacco."

"You what, now? Svea smokes?"

Rolf cracks a high laugh and slaps Willy on the thigh, slap and laugh both discomfiting his own achy head. "Not Svea, Taavi!"

"Bejaazus, man!"

"Well, you seem quite cozy with that Taavi, whereas Svea is the changeling witch who will throw your mojo back in your face like the trout."

"Mojo! Ach, Rolf, you are a lot smarter than you look, you young bugger, and I can see escaping from your sister has been a major preoccupation your whole life!"

"I want you to know, I did not expect her to be here. Well . . . "

"But she was, you fibber. And I am . . . "

"Hooked? Maybe you can get over it with Dottirsmor."

"Rolf, mon."

"You think you are hurting? My head is a son-of-a-bitch. I cannot drink like you and those Hollanders."

"It would be a beautiful day if we could see it through headache and heartache."

"Do you remember last night, what you did?"
"Yes, I drank a lot, but I think I was not so drunk . . . remember everything, mostly."

"And?"

"I will apologize to your father, but I will take back nothing."

"So you are still not exactly sober."

"Yes, I am sober." Though I may be bleeding to death. Your grandmother's Norns are drinking my blood.

"So then, tell me about Taavi, for the distraction. She is a widow, yes?"

"Husband was at least half Lapp, and her too, I think. Her name, it is male, you know, a Finnish form of David, which was her husband's name, or one of them, I think he had several. They published together, and somehow she ended up with just the Taavi, with some title like Doctor, at first. Husband was at least half Lapp, and her too, I think. There was a Sami partisan group in the last war with a mysterious leader named Taavi who may have been one or both of them at different times. He lived some of the time as teacher with those who were Russian serfs on Kola peninsula, some in Murmansk in Russian administration, a spy, in a word, and historian of the people at the same time. They were—what do you say?—prominent historians and exiles, complicated people who maybe once knew Lenin, and others wandering in and out. I do not know how they escaped the purges. And then Finland, England. I guess they spent a sabbatical year or some time in your Australia. Then he went a bit crazy, was put away, and died in an asylum here. I remember him slightly, silent. What do you call it, bit of an . . . ogre? Farmor thought they were both, err, refugee spies, and we did not have much to do with them before she died. Now, Far has become a friend to Taavi, but to me she is still intimidating, a wizard or something. She looks as if she could still carry a sword, and has lived through many wars, and been in more than one prison, I think."

"I think she is tremendous. I understand how you might have been afraid of her until you were, say, five, but . . . Surely having her as neighbor is like, say, Linnaeus living over there."

"Linné! So you know of him."

"Of course. I am a geologist and all that. He was not quite Darwin, but he was one of the giants, the great classifier. Hey, did I ever tell you I stayed the first night in Uppsala in the Hotel Linné?"

"Your astrology is, shall we say, full of . . . odd things."

***

When Rolf and Willy go into the shop after tying up the canoe with the fishing gear still in it, Frans is asking Bengt, over coffee (fresh from the house in honor of the guests), if he gets much local traffic.

"Dalarna is depopulated. It does not have the people density." Frans muses, "A higher density of ghosts than people. Ah, here are the heroes back from the wars, the population rises again. Did you catch any fish?"

"A few small ones. I will put them in the freezer for Far."

Bengt acknowledges this with small wave of the hand, offers coffee to the two younger men, with curious beetling smile for Willy.

"Yes," continues Bengt to Frans, "and I am not one of those fifth-generation businesses on a main street. Because we are not in town, it takes deliberation to get in a car and come for no purpose,

121

different from the pedestrian days when people just dropped in off the street without intent. Someone will bring an old coat hook to match, and it is felt to be payment enough to share an old anecdote about a former neighbor. So, I have a fill of trivial job work, though much of it is not easy, and a burden of gossip like a barber, which is a tax and impedes work on paying jobs. It is different from the barber's, of course. They will stay longer and just watch if you hammer hard and fast, but it is difficult to draw and measure while the uncles recount how the horses bolted down the field and dragged Yngve Frey in the traces so he never walked again, and it is a mistake to ask, Now, when was that?

"One might say an historian should draw these people out," with a low look at the chair where Taavi sat some hours ago, "or run a tape recorder, but that would be another life, and want a blacksmith to work while the historian quibbled with the guests about the veracity of their recollection, and it would be unsatisfactory for all, it seems to me.

"I am glad to see them and listen, but soon enough impatient for them to leave. At least they never ask me much about my life, because I was merely an engineer, of the same caste as the priest and doctor, not of the land, and not from the district. I sometimes go to Johannson's works in Nyköping for help, and it is different there. The brothers came into their father's father's business, and so they have authority of the old times, and they keep it an industrial place, no spectators. Of course, they have apprentices and discipline. And there is vigor, you know, and coordination which I do not have.

"If this workshop were in Gävle it would be a tourist spectacle and unworkable. As it is, I am somewhat a district secret and find real work through a thin network of informers. Or informants, is it?"

"Damn," says Frans to Rolf, "never have I heard such a long speech in Dalarna! Perhaps the gate is stuck in the mud of a hangover!"

"Perhaps," says Joost, "he has been rehearsing a sermon all night."

"That Svea went on about mosquitoes last night," says Rolf, and immediately regrets reference to last night, which he and Willy have avoided for several almost-silent hours on the lake this morning.

"Yes, but she is recently in the mode of lecturing epidemiologists," says Frans.
"A fine capacity in a fiancée," says Joost, because, of course, they cannot all leave it alone; it is still lying there with the couple of *brännvin* bottles which did not get picked up yet.

Willy sucks in a deep breath: "Her father has not yet given permission."

Joost laughs, and slaps Willy on the back. "The knight in motley has sworn his dedication to the lady of the lake, if the King will have it!"

Bengt says, "The aspirin is over there, Willy. Have some coffee with it."

Frans asks Rolf, "So what time did you get out there on the lake? Did you see any of the children of old mother Gädda?"

"We both snored, did not sleep well, and were up at dawn. The big fish are still all asleep or extinct, or very well fed, anyway."

Willy pats the anvil as they go by. "Your second wife?" he asks Bengt.

Bengt laughs. "I put dirt around the base to quieten it, do you see? But this one, perhaps, does relieve the other of a lot of conversation."

***

A small bell rings at the house, and Adela calls, "Breakfast is out!" Willy bows his head, and would prefer to go last, but Frans insists he goes in front, after Rolf. Here it comes. Quick, rehearse, what. Apology! Argh!

A whopping Swedish breakfast is laid out: sliced meats and cheeses, breads, berries, coffee. The eye gets lost. The real smörgåsbord. Svea is occupied making juice and another coffee pot. Willy has heard of such breakfasts but has never been subjected to one: a breakfast that will last a work day, as they say. Pleasantries are exchanged, but it is evident that people are avoiding looking at the cloud that is or should be over Willy's head. He is not at all hungry, although the other men busily load up plates and coffee cups.

"I have something to say."

"Ah, well, Willy." It is a gentle offer from Adela to blame it on the *brännvin*.

"I apologize to everyone for being uncouth last night. But I do not take it back. Any of it."

"Willy, it has not been so common for the last century or so for a man to barter in public for a woman like livestock," says Bengt unsmilingly. Svea is looking on Willy to see him crack, now.

"Of course. You must understand that I asked permission to woo Svea out of reverence for her entire family, not to buy her."

Adela says with a twinkle, "Willy, this is still very unconventional. But since you have sought to woo her in public, you should continue to do so, if you are serious about both her, our Svea, and our permission, as you say. How do you propose to proceed?"

Everybody is wolfing down food now, on chairs drawn back from the laden table. Willy has taken a bowl of blueberries, is it, and Rolf has poured *filmjölk* on top. Willy knows what *filmjölk* is—fermented milk—through mistaken purchases at the grocery store, and hates it. Good God, how can they drink that shit? And Rolf knows it. Willy holds the bowl now in penitence before him. He notes that Rolf, well, Frans too, and Joost, seem to be relishing the entertainment, which is to be the roasting of Willy.

Willy clears his throat and says, "I would like to request an audience with the lady Svea on the lakeshore path. After breakfast, of course. Allowing whomever wishes to accompany us as chaperones. For I have no secrets; I am defenseless before, um." But he thinks, Jesus, where did this script come from?
"Splendid!" says Frans. "Joost and I will bring the coffee pot and perhaps some champagne. And now, to be serious, how about the bride price?"

"I, er, the bride price?"

"I think that should be set by the bride, ah, the person of interest," says Bengt, "though payable to me, of course. Five years of servitude might be a good start."

"What does the lady Svea say at this point in the negotiation?" asks Joost.

"This has little enough to do with me," says Svea icily. That crimps the humor all round.

Perhaps that entertainment is not properly rehearsed, is the feeling, coffee cups rattle and the pot is passed. Oh, *howabout the weather* is about to surface.

"Nonetheless," insists Willy, "I do humbly request the audience, if it please you, Svea, for it is altogether about you."

"You mock yourself so well, I do not think you need anyone to share the task."

"Not just anyone. I beg you to share it with me."

"As a free woman, I ask you to stay out of my path."

"As a free man, I ask you to measure whether two might not walk abreast on your path."

"Perhaps you should walk with everyone else, and Fram and I should walk behind with the ass and the ox."

"If I could be your ass, I would be happy to walk with you and Fram. I am sure your ox would be very nice too."
"If you were not so plain an ass, Fram would bite yours."
"That would be backward of Fram, since I slipped him tidbits last night."

"One cannot trust that you understand your own puns, Willy, or how sincere you are, or even if you are whole and not mad. In fact, the contrary is evident."

"I know *Fram* was Amundsen's icebreaker, and Nansen's, that it means 'forward.' I am wholly sincere, and the madness, well, everybody has at least one bad habit. I may have more than the average ass."

"Usch, Willy. Willy-willy. I think you are causing yourself much pain going through this, this drama, and in front of everyone, by your mad ramblings. Your eyes are bleeding. Do you have a plastic sword to fall on? No? No silly props other than the ass?"

"Walk with me and let our asses follow or not, as they will."

"May we come, after all?" shriek Joost and Rolf, almost in chorus. "No, not until after breakfast!" says Adela. Glances at the table, food still aplenty, but plates passing back and forth like swallows, animating the performance, everyone an actor. And how the food is vanishing!

Svea walks out the door, Willy in close pursuit, and now, perhaps, they are out of earshot. Svea murmurs, "But, Willy, what do you really want?"

She moves to brush a bug from the back of her wrist, and in that moment Willy grasps her hand lightly. Reflexively she curls her grip around his thumb and they stand like that, an apologetic stammer stuck in his throat, but a galvanic cool warmth flushes from the contact, startling both of them. Holy!

He whispers, "Hold fast!", and she does for five seconds, and then gently lifts his hand and puts it down.

"Say something!" says Willy.

"But there is nothing to say to you! You are a fool and trying to speak simply to you leads to absurdities."

Her nostrils flare, if she smoked now she would be a dragon.

Svea went on, "And here you are walking into the ruins of my childhood and you say, *say something*, as if you are offering me a small role in your drama. *Oh look! Here come Willy and Svea from around the lake with moonberries!*"

Willy stares at her, her eyes flash flames, bubble of sputum on her bitten lip, wonders at himself, what has happened to him that he has the balls to mount this pyre. Clearly I am mad, have mercy on me!

"There are no moonberries out there of course. Far walks the forest for miles and has bottled every one except tomorrow's, which may spring from where he has pissed."

Suddenly the telephone rings inside, and someone holds the door open so that Svea and Willy hear. Everyone listens as Adela answers, speaking loudly for the venerable Taavi on the other end of the phone who has fallen, does not think she is badly hurt, but asks if Adela or Rolf could come help her, and if the clinic insists she come in, if someone might drive her, very sorry. Adela says she will come immediately, Adela can take her to town.

There is a chill as Adela and Bengt leave. Rolf is loath to move, spellbound.

"Taavi is a terrific person," offers Joost. "One hopes she is all right. A bit elderly, with not-so-good eyesight, living alone, it could go badly."

"She is a sturdy old wench," says Frans, "who has weathered more trials and grief than any one person could be expected to. I expect she will be back here with them in no time, to supervise this drama, as soon as she finds her glasses. Though, a fall at her age is a concern?"

"I think," says Svea, "that Willy already feels Taavi and Fram are his allies in this madness, what you call this drama, and I think I am going to go for a drive. Alone." And trips down the drive, clumsily. She has no keys on her person, so she gets in Bengt's old square Volvo army surplus Laplander truck, in which keys are superfluous. Willy grabs and pulls himself into the bed as she turns in the drive and goes by. Does she see him do this? At the top of the drive, she looks directly at him in the mirror, and stops.

"Damnit!" she shouts. So Willy gets down and stands at the rear wheel. He waits to see, will she wait for him or speed off. She pauses, and he slips around into the passenger seat.

"Be quiet!"

Willy was not about to say a word, and besides, the Laplander sounds like ten of Rolf's Saab woodchoppers when she lets the clutch out and a ton and a half of loosely tied steel goes into a hundred frequencies of chafing and jiggling and flapping and growling, bobbing and conversing with the forest and the gravel road. There is a highly polished knob with an amber stone in it clamped on the steering wheel, which she holds as if she once made it. Oh, thinks Willy, fucking oh, it deepens.

She turns onto the road and drives down the middle for a mile, then into an old track which enters a pine plantation. Stops in the darkness of their shadow. Scots pines, is it? Do I get out and go around to open her door? Only follow. She looks straight ahead for half a minute, idling, then turns off the engine and gets out.

"Willy."

"Uh."

"Your performance has been remarkable. I am not sure I kept up to you all the time, the language thing. But now . . . Now you must stop. It is . . . very silly. You know nothing about me. Are you campaigning for the Bergström estate, and I am one of the attached serfs? Willy, you are a stupid foreigner with a handicap, an idiot. I am going to leave you here to walk back, and I will go to Stockholm." Finally, she looks him in the face, eyes black, burning. "What am I to you, an excuse for a fit, is it?"

"What it is, I *recognized* you."

"You *recognized* me? What in hell is that?" This is shrill, a whispered shriek.

"Okay, you are a magpie duchess, the royal *skata*, that has lost its awdle oodle ardle and doesn't know it."

"Hah!" It is half a laugh, half wondering.

Willy touches her chin, and says, "You Swedes do not laugh easily, your funny bone is atrophied."

"Atrophied. Well, perhaps you think you will teach me some new words and to laugh suitably."

"Your sarcasm—what is it called?— at any rate, it is a start. On laughter."

"And when you have taught me all these useful skills then . . . "

"Then I can take you home to your mother and father for their approval!"

Now she laughs. "Willy, you are odd. Where does this come from, is it your drugs?"

"I am not, perhaps, the tall blond knight on a white horse you were expecting."

"Why do you think I was, am, waiting on anyone? I am not a figure in your fairy story."

Wait, wait. Let the fly and the bee speak their turn in the dapple, the butterfly nod on the grass head, and the birdies fluff on the higher branches. This is the way the world trips along.

"Willy, when I was a child I dreamed, like a child, a lot of strange things. I grew out of those."

Willy says, "On the lake this morning, I was imagining your childhood here, jealous of Fram." He lifts his hand and brushes a dog hair from her shoulder, and fingertips almost touch the clavicle, the blaze. They stand like that, breath held; an eddy of air breathes for them. Oh.

"Willy, you are in a romantic hangover."

"It doesn't matter what you call it. Here is the postcard Dalarna, thrilling, but then came you. And . . . "

They look upon each another. Her mouth and eyes are wide open.

"You are a lunatic!" Too loud, then repeating in a whisper, "You are a lunatic." Oh, but her eyes are wet. "Goodbye . . ."

She strides to the Laplander and starts it, and backs down the path. Soon she is receding in a rattle. Willy listens to Dalarna a minute, then walks to the road. His pulse is a thunderstorm, his feet are slow to rediscover the rhythm of walking, the hook pulls at every step like a grapnel tied to a sinking ship.

***

"Sorry I am late, Birgit and friends! A long run yesterday, slept in, and badly!"

"I told everyone else earlier, Willy, we are all going to Stockholm next Monday on buses, to tour some outstanding sights of the city. Here is a copy of the notice for you. Be sure to come on time, shake the sand out tonight, yes?"

***

Knock, knock. "Rolf."

"Yes. I am studying, as you can hear. Football. Liverpool is not on the TV today, so it is the radio." Rolf is wearing this team scarf and pompom beanie. Even stranger, thinks Willy, here in his room with the radio than in front of the basement TV.

Willy studies the short wave radio. Ah, ask later, but now: "Would you please do something for me?"

"Uh oh, is it the police again?"

"Brother Rolf. Could you please call Svea for me?"

"Oh, damn, Willy, I am strongly regretting taking you home. Why don't you go ask Morsdottir for her mother's number?"

"Rolf, it is very different."

"Hear me, I doubt she will be home."

"But try, eh?"

They go to the common phone down by the entrance; Willy slouches into the kitchen to make some space for Rolf to speak, if she answers. Someone answers. *Aue*, what if not her? "Just talk to him," he hears Rolf say, twice.

"Here you are."

"Hello, Willy. You wanted to talk to me?"
'Yes, no. I want to see you."

"Well, that is not so easy. You are there and I am here."
"I could bike on down there."

"*Dumpsch*. Willy-Willy."

"*Je tu en pris*?"

"Perhaps we might go, then, to the opera on Saturday," she says after a breath.

"Where?"

"Stockholm. Just come by train and I will meet you at the station, tell Rolf when. Perhaps it is the *Zauberflöte*. Of course, you will have to rent a suit."

She hangs up. He listens to the dead phone, eyes crunched. Rolf comes out of the kitchen as he hangs up the receiver and starts back toward his room.

Rolf calls, "Willy."

Willy turns. Rolf sees the face is not defeated as he could have expected, it is some sort of, what, berserk Buddha there."Rolf, it is not your fault."
What now? thinks Rolf.

"Hey, do you happen to have a suit?"

"God help us," Rolf whispers.

Yes, it should be, *Je t'en pris.*

***

 # The Lads

They were none of them charged with anything other than disturbing the peace, just held for a few hours, IDs checked, shuffled from check-in to a succession of holding rooms, hearing potential charges of rowdiness, vandalism, kicking over trash cans, littering, and observed through sobering up from whatever they were on. Then they were kicked out, charges dropped, singly into the gray dawn. The first was sitting on the curb nursing his head and wondering how soon the buses would run, when the second came out the same door. Each was unsure if the other had been at the same party, not buds anyway, so they stood at some remove and stared at each other. Too beat to fight anyhow unless obliged. The first grunted and dusted his jacket, and looked for insignia on the second; there were none though some shadows where they might have been once.

They were about to turn and go in diametrically opposite shuffles without a word, when a third came out, and both stopped to see who it might be. Number three called, "Otto!", and the first two waited for him to come up to them. "Jens," said the first, "well at least it was warmer in there."

"Who is this *snubbe* then?"

They were none of them charged with anything other than disturbing the peace, just held for a few hours, IDs checked, shuffled from check-in to a succession of holding rooms, hearing potential charges of rowdiness, vandalism, kicking over trash cans, littering, and observed through sobering up from whatever they were on. Then they were kicked out, charges dropped, singly into the gray dawn. The first was sitting on the curb nursing his head and wondering how soon the buses would run, when the second came out the same door. Each was unsure if the other had been at the same party, not buds anyway, so they stood at some remove and stared at each other. Too beat to fight anyhow unless obliged. The first grunted and dusted his jacket, and looked for insignia on the second; there were none though some shadows where they might have been once.

They were about to turn and go in diametrically opposite shuffles without a word, when a third came out, and both stopped to see who it might be. Number three called, "Otto!", and the first two waited for him to come up to them. "Jens," said the first, "well at least it was warmer in there."

"Who is this *snubbe* then?"

"Dunno. Were you at the party at Ingrid's?"

"I dunno any Ingrid. I was with a band."

"That band was shit!"

"Well they were shit-faced, fucked up."

"Yeah, and loud without being exactly musical. Some bad gräss too man, think laced with some serious toxic shit. You get that crashing thing, like an implosion?"

"Nah, I did not do any of that, had my own stuff."

"Yeah? Did you know that shit was toxic?"

Belligerent stares. "At least it wore off. I slept standing up in there some."

"Me too. Bastards came in and poked me though when the eyes closed."

"Here comes another."

This one in denim, with sneakers, in contrast to the first three, all in black leather and shit-kicking hobnail boots.

"Hej Otto. Who is this? Bud?"

"Not yet. He was with the band. If it was the same party."

"What's your handle mate?"

"Sven. I nivver seen these guys before, not at any party neither."

"Ah well. Ending up at same exit though. But I am Sven, you can be something else if you wanna be in this group."

"Who says?"

"I say; I am Sven, you can be, ah, Tintin?"

"What now? I ain't gonna be nobody's poodle!"

"OK, keep your hair on, you can come up with your own thing. Christ, that was crap back there, not even a lousy coffee, let's go down the road and see if summat's open. S'pose you are all broke. Never mind. Who wants a fag?"

"*Gossar* wanna go for a ride?"

"Ride? What for?"

"Support Swedish Rail, you know? And a little action, some

good money! Speak up normal-like lads, don't wanna look like a whispering conspiracy, eh?"

"What action then? I was supposed to start a job."

"OK. Anyone wants out, go now. Got about a one week gig, then we all free, flush."

"Well, tell us."

"What about you, Tintin?"

"Well fock."

"OK, go on home to Mama. Boys 'n me, we got a gig. Right, Otto, Jens?"

"Wait, I'm in, maybe, just don't call me Tintin."

"OK Tintin. Here's the deal. We take a train ride, meet a guy with a yacht, sail on back to Amsterdam, become a band with some guitar cases and all, pack some shit onto the yacht, and bring it back to some port to be determined, as they say, distribute it."

"Whaaat? Sounds like a setup. Well, don't it?"

"Yeah, we are too conspicuous."

"Well that's the guts of it, yes? You stay in your leathers, strut it, wear a little lipstick even, like your purple shirt Tintin, and you are a band, shout a little village Danish, cops up there will avoid us, break no law and they will stay the hell away like you have plague."

"So why does the yacht not just pick us up here, dammit?"

"Cause it is already in port, owner is laid back, visiting museums, fancy restaurants, all that bourgee shit, and does not want to make a bunch of stops and checks, you know? And like, those in on it do not need to be making side visits to Granny, and once you are paid, do what in hell you want, eh? Look, you already said you were in, but you know nothing, you do not need to trust anyone, it just goes ker-ching, ker-ching and then we are done. Not saying, there would not be another."

"Sounds like a fairy tale."

"Yeah, could fall apart if you turned out to actually be musical, become celebrities, right?"

"So why me?"

"Right Tintin, we need a drummer eh! And there you are, call it fate, that you got shoved out at the same time as the rest of us!"

"Fate is bullshit, shit just happens."

"Exactly my friend, fate is shit that happens. And as it happens this Otto cannot play a guitar but he can carry a case. Here comes someone else out that door, let's go find some damn aspirin."

So all let the Sven lead off down the pavement, disheveled but with some sort of authority in the raised collar and green shoe laces, and the bidding, *Come*.

***

So here they are, four nonce names, off to Stockholm on the train. Getting out, they are impressed by the capital architecture, shitloads of capitalist masonry. Sven goes to a meeting in a coffee shop, tells the others to follow the main street east out of the station, and south to the river, and meet him there at a taxi stop at the Opera House. Know how to find south, no? So the boys go east and end up in Sergelstorg, the big non-square with construction mess, and go north up Sveagatan a block or two before they realize the shadows are wrong, and do an about turn and go on back toward Gustav II Adolphus square.

They peer over the river there, a low roar, how long is that Sven gonna be with his taxi, the statue of the guy on the horse is pointing over the river at, what, the government building it seems, makes Otto a bit nervous, what's the focker lookin' at. Busses unloading tourists over there, looks like.

"Some sailboats downriver there, on both banks. Let's walk along the bank just a ways and take a look, he'll find us."

***

Chapter 7

Stockholm

Willy is standing outside the capital's train station on Vasagatan with small duffel bag on the shoulder and the suit in another over his arm. The train was one minute late, according to the platform clock. He waits. He paces for ten minutes, looking about, being conspicuous. Then he understands this is either a stand-up or a test, or both. And so, he stands unmoving, heart sinking between his knees, head bowed, waiting for what will come, humiliation or, well, a turn of the tide. His mind becomes periglacial, granite pavers soak his soles with a little alpha and gamma radiation, his bones pause the continuous maintenance, his heart feels to be a crow cawing in a tree. People move around him as if he were a statue, waves coming from this arriving train and that, and a steady trickle in the other direction, into the station. Loud and quiet, by turns. Oh.

Ten minutes he has stood unmoving, when he sees her coming. He sees her from afar and sees that she has been watching him for some time. The crow launches from the tree. She stands in front of him, at a judicious distance, and looks at and through him, and finally engages his gaze.

"Here I am," he says. In ruin, actually, so that he is not even clear what language he is in. Two days of anticipatory self-immolation and then this blast freeze. Nothing more suave rises. Afraid to say anything; listen then. Spook said I am not a good listener.

"So you are." And, "Come, idiot."

She walks in front, but then slows and he comes up to her shoulder. Shoulder to shoulder.

"*Zauberflöte,*" he says. "Dim princelet given a flute by a Queen of the Cockatoos to get her daughter back. Turns out she is kidnapped by divorced father, who has taken up with a Masonic Lodge, but who will trade daughter for a couple of tunes." Whoa, he thinks, curb it. His body is jolted at the touch of shoulders, front to back.

"You know it so well!"

"Have only heard bits on the radio as a youth. Can whistle some of the tunes and not make sense of the story, except guy gets girl. Happy, I mean happily. Tough for that Queen."

"Willy, you are trying to make me laugh. Should I laugh?"

"I think a token of appreciation for my trying would be nice, but I am patient."

"So, it was somewhat civilized for you to hear *Zauberflöte* on the radio."

"Ah, it tried to be. Radio modeled itself on the BBC foreign service: speak wisely to your peoples and they will love your wisdom. Once a day the "Air on G-string" would introduce a bass voice— "Readings from the Bible,"—and ponderously delivered the catch of the day. One day, I realized the readings were getting sillier each time. Deeply into the gibberish of the Psalms, deliver my mail unto the Philistines, and on the eighth day throw out the parrot and drink the water. Someone was subverting it."

"Willy, your Swedish is entertaining, but now your English is not understandable to me. I think you get a bit possessed. Could you try to speak sense a little?"

So, quiet; they listen to themselves not speaking, and he to the currents of her breathing under it, between their steps, clip phit, clip phit. Prayer of an atheist for a modicum of grace: don't let me trip.

"And your French, *c'est execrable*. You must have hated your French teacher."

Turns out, she does not have tickets to the opera. Turns out, it is not in season. They walk past the opera house. Svea is unapologetic. The test is still running, apparently.

"So then, we should eat something."

Sitting in a sandwich shop on Sveagatan, for god's sake, on stools, she says, "Willy, you know nothing about me. I think you somehow imagine I am a book where you will learn who you are."

"If you mean . . . If it is a question of my being a, a serious person or, um, just a vagrant. I have some money, I have . . . "

"And you think because I am blemished that I should be grateful to come into your garden with your little jokes?"

"Blemished! Ah. Not. Your face, may I touch it?"

"No."

"Well, may I kiss you?"

"No."

"He was de-spi-sed, despised and rejected, and acquainted with grief!"

Now she laughs. "Handel also. Perhaps you can sing in that choir, the Mormons, when you wander off to Utah."

"If I were religious, I would pray to be spared that Utah."

"You do not have to be religious to be a Mormon, according to Laxness—just a bit simple."

"I do not know this . . . Laxness, is it?"

"You should. He is an Icelander who won the Nobel Prize for literature. He wrote one book maybe ten years ago about Icelanders going to Utah to become Mormons. Right, how do you say it, up your street. You might find yourself at home there. You could have several wives to take care of you."

"Svea, why did you meet me? I know you stood back there looking for some time before you decided to come to fetch me, after all."

She looks down at the floor for the longest five seconds. Her face is unguarded when she looks back up at him and says, "Perhaps I wanted a Papageno for the weekend. Now, we must walk. Far."

***

Right inside the door, standing against coats, Willy kisses Svea, so tentatively and gently she thinks he is afraid. He is holding his breath, she feels. He takes her hand and leads her to the hard couch he can see from the door and bids her lie face-down on it, with a cushion under her cheek. Then he takes off her shoes and massages her feet, near five minutes each, through stockings, big toe to heel. He presses firmly with thumb, melting into knotty sole, and back; then middle toe to heel and back, then little toe to the outside of the heel. When he has done each foot, he gives the sole a sharp slap and lays the foot down. At first bewildered, she asks him where he learned this, but then she lets herself drift away with it.

142

When he is done with the feet, he kneels by her midriff and goes to work with thumbs on her shoulders, supra-clavicle to the knots on the shoulder blade, and then underneath along the sides of her spine. Then he sits back on his heels beside her.

Svea turns, lays her hand on his shoulder, and regards him. Then she says, "Willy, are you trying to make me comfortable with you, or are you just afraid of me?"

"I am lost." In fact, the only one in the room who seems to have an idea of the plot is his hard-on, which transubstantiates all the longing of his life into rock.

In the room, which he has begun to notice, an eyeless African mask is watching them. On the low table is a pile of papers and text books, and a coffee cup. Svea leans over him to pick up the coffee cup and pours the cold lees on his thigh. He crunches, and waits for the lightning to follow.

"Damn, Willy, you dress like, like, a foreigner. One cannot tell if you are tolerable-looking in a satanic way or ugly as hell."

I am bewildered, he thinks. What did she do?

"Dammit, Willy, get up and out of those clothes and shower. I will bring you a towel."

***

"Willy, perhaps you should go now."

"Said the princess to the plumber."

"Devil. You are going to be a shit about this, yes?"

"Yes!"

"What do you think you are? You are a foreigner, a gypsy, an idiot.

143

Everything you say is messed up like a bomb blast, your feet are thorn bushes, and your eyebrows grow together."

"No they don't."

"Hah!"

"Come look in the mirror." Pulls her, resisting slightly, toward the small entry mirror. She looks, wrapped in a sheet. He looks at her looking. He points his finger at her in the mirror, halfway to her image.

"Girl pulls shutters and tells boy to go away. Boy says through shutters, 'Go look in the mirror and count to five; and then come open the shutters and kiss me again.'"

"You think I am supposed to see the unborn tribe of Australian Viking boys heaving the longboat to the water, and to melt? I think I read that story."

"You saw that!"

"Oh, Willy. You are an idiot and an . . . "

He moves to kiss her shoulder, and she bends her head to touch his with the tiniest bump, while seeing herself, themselves, in the glass.

"Remember the feather?"

"What feather?"

"Me too."

"Caught off balance, both of us."

"But you resolved that . . . "

"What?"

"That nothing happened; it was a sneeze."

"Yes. No."

"May I say . . ."

"What? No!"

***

"Willy, tell me something honest, true."

"Eighty kilos, one hundred and seventy-eight centimeters . . . No, not that. So what, perhaps . . . like something bad I did, rather than just happening to me, for which I am eternally ashamed?"

"I did not say what color."

"Just . . . *honest*?"

"Hmm."

"Well. Australia has a national anthem, you know, a song, god and queen stuff, but in the beginning it was transported convicts, the English competing with the Belgians to be the vilest colonial nation. So there is a vein, you understand, not a subculture but a folk notion of the victim and the antihero, like Ned Kelly, the Irish bank robber who made a last stand against the police, also Irish, wearing armor forged from boilers I think. And the prospectors, like that P Mack, most of who died of thirst in the outback, just a few finding Eurekas and Golden Miles. And a third of Australians actually think the national anthem is 'Waltzing Matilda', about a tramp who nabs a sheep and is bailed up by the squatter, an Englishman who grafted his way into a government land grant. The swagman, he is called, for the roll of his belongings carried on the back, drowns himself in a waterhole rather than spending the rest of his life in jail over an English sheep.

"I cannot say they are my people, Mack and Kelly and the swagman, I worked for a corporation after all. If I had been one of them I would be dead in the bush. But . . . "

"So you are a sheep thief at heart who would rather wake up in a Swedish bed than in prison. Or perhaps you have stolen a Swedish girl and are pleading insanity?"

"Yes, all of the above, I only plead for mercy on account of she was a flirt!"

"What is a flirt? Ah. No mercy for you! Damn! Now I am going to shower; by myself this time. And while I do that you will go to the store to get us breakfast: out the door, left, then right two streets."

But while she is in the shower Willy tears a few pages out of the back of one of her lecture note pads, takes some crayons from a bowl and quickly drafts four cartoons from Waltzing Matilda. When she comes out, she asks, "What did you get?"

"Ah. I did not go in fact, I drew these for you instead. I wanted to walk to the store with you, hand-in-hand, like lovers."

She frowns, shuffles the loose pages, and says, "I see you are something of an artist, as well as a sheep thief. You can tell me the story when we get back. Perhaps you can be trained to buy groceries, but then this time you will need the hands to hold the basket."

***

Walking side by side, she avoids taking his hand, and says, "So now, my face."

Willy tenses. Oh shit, now I am on trial. For my life, is it.

"I did not even know Rolf had a sister," he begins. "And when you stepped into the light out of that dark shop I was stunned. I saw a fiery angel, in armor. I thought you might be a celestial being. But then I saw the dog loved you, that Fram, and perhaps you were mortal. When I stood beside you smelling that same soap I use, brushing your hand, I thought perhaps I could learn from Fram. Though looking into your face I thought Fram must be quite brave, and I was just an alien klutz and not Siegfried, was I having a fit I wondered, but no, I was somewhere else, it was the fire on the mountain."

"That was perhaps evasive, Mr. not-Siegfried. Now be quiet and hold this basket."

Wenz thought it something to flaunt, her blaze. Aida at Wien opera: black velvet dress he bought her, bare throat, exotic princess out of the frozen north on his tuxedo arm, weathering stares from under tiaras (maybe there were no tiaras or monocles?) and beetle brows. She flushing, petulance rising. An itch spreading red from the shoulders, and evolving to ferocity, all the buried savagery of the problem child she once was, crushing Wenz and blasting her out of orbit. Followed by indignant discovery of pregnancy, an abortion. Then running into, not running to, Adela in a Stockholm park, ungluing, not quite to abject collapse, but a flood of emotion in torrents of anger, eddies of recrimination, plunging angst under scudding tears: Mor! But none of that for Willy's confidence.

***

Walking back, she said, "Willy! Now I will tell you my side. At first you were amusing, you were making everyone laugh that night, then we argued a bit, and it amused them, the others, to provoke us, and then you did the kneeling thing. Good god! I was horrified! Hell Willy, I do not need or want a husband or protector, and on you came like a mad dog! I saw though that you were compelled and horrified yourself, even if you were play-acting. I was fascinated, is that the word? You were berserk and defenseless at the same time, yes, an idiot - Myshkin! Were you after all very drunk? Yes, I ran out.

147

I did not sleep, I walked along the road. Then in the morning they were all, as it were, pushing me to accept a contract or something, hilarious, no? No! I was afraid of you then. So I left. Just a small tornado in Dalarna, I said, now just to let it blow away. And then the damned Opera, what was I thinking?"

"Which was not in season, as you well knew,' whispered Willy. "But to which I brought Rolf's suit, which was probably too tight for me!"

"And after getting in my bed once you think I am going to give you a key! You . . . sheep thief!"

"So what do you think your Norns intend for us?"

"Boy-toy for a weekend. Goddamit Willy you know I have no time for that stuff, gods and fairies!"

"But were you not the *näck* child?"

"Once I was a child. Perhaps you were not, Willy."

"Now I will tell you something. Only you must listen and not interrupt." She pauses, looking gravely downward into some past. Willy waits, not breathing. After a bit she begins to speak, in Swedish.

 "When Rolf was born, Farmor came to live with us for a time. She came from Norrbotten. Mor used to say Far was a changeling, do you understand that word bortbyting? Well there is no room in my bed for a tourist, you can figure it out or not. Meaning, she could not have been his real mother. "

Now her voice drops in register and the accent shifts and becomes strange to him, rolling, the voice of Norrlanders who speak little and ponder long how to use fewer words, and some of those words are new to him.

"Much of the time she spoke little but when we were alone she

148

became somebody else and lectured me. She said I was marked by the näck folk and protected by them. She said I would have to protect this brother and other children. She said I would not need a man to protect me or a prince like some of those German stories. That if I wanted to test it I should wish for an Icelandic pony, and if one came she would take care of it."

Willy realizes he is hearing a performance out of an old vault and he needs to listen more than to understand.

"Willy I did not wish for a half crazy foreigner. Or the pony; but perhaps you are the split-hoofed punishment they sent, she sent.

"When you said you recognized me, you remember, in Dalarna, obviously you were gibbering; but afterwards, I thought, well, perhaps I would have to kill you."

"Okay," says Willy, unsure.

"Okay! You are a total idiot Willy! If only you would sleep a little I could do it!"

The exclamation frees Willy from his incomprehension, and he laughs and touches her chin. Her mouth opens and she glares; and then snorts, and giggles.

Well, thinks Willy, that was a dark cave but I think we are through it for now!

***

When they come back in the door Willy thinks to make a fresh start. "So then tell me, did you grow up in that house?"

"No. At first we were in Gävle." She takes the offered path.

"And?"

"We, they, bought that place in Dalarna and went there on weekends. For a few years, I went to high school in Avesta. Willy, you do not talk about your childhood either."

"I grew up under an active volcano, and the sky was always gray with ash and loud with pterodactyls—nothing memorable."

"You should give me the name of your resumé writer. I lacked only the volcano."

"You are three or four years older than Rolf?"

"Almost four. I did bully him as a child. I bullied everyone. Then I had a very boring and not happy or unhappy adolescence, and then was a sulking teenager, until . . . "

"Until you were formally introduced to Monsewer Mosquito."

"Yes, you could say. Epidemiology. First in Uppsala, then in Stockholm. Then research, conferences in Edinburgh and Wien." And Wenz and his scholarship, conferences and opera: a bright stable for a country filly.

"Rolf said there was a prof."

"Ah, Rolf said. Do you know what he said about you?"

"Oops. Of course, I did not know he wanted me to tame his elder sister."

"That was not kind, Willy."

"So you were in Uppsala."

"The place where you and Rolf live at Flogsta was not there then. I lived in student housing near the university. You might think we are all Swedes and one people, so to say, but I was a provincial girl and belonged to Uplands student nation. I was bad tempered, and

a bad student in a rowdy lot, until the mosquito bit, as you say it."
He missed that mention of Avesta high school. She is relieved not
to have to explain. Not exactly expelled, but advised to make a
fresh start.

A longish silence. Then, suddenly, he tips her chin and kisses her on
the blaze—top, middle, slowly. Then where it stops on the collar
bone. Too quick for her to jerk away, too measured to object. Too.
Hush. Into this hush might fall . . . a tear? A fart.

"Vandal!"

"At least I do not have to translate it."

***

"At first glance I took you for a refugee hitchhiker. Still not sure!"

"I thought you were a Valkyrie."

"But you asked Far to be my husband, more or less!"

"Yes!"

"Well the Valkyrie would be our Norns, and they are known for
going to battlefields and taking slain warriors away to Valhalla."

"Fair enough, just when you get there we can change the story.
That is why it is a story!"

"You mean, Willy, a quick divorce and, ah, off to Utah."

"Ha, I'd rather go with you to Valhalla, Waltzing Matilda! Only, how
many warriors will you take in?"

"You can count the helmets!"

***

"What do you call this?" she asked.

"That? You mean, do I give it a name, like John Thomas, in Lady Chatterley?"

"Do you?"

"No. My mother might have called it my willy when I was a tweeker. So it could be Willy's willy."
"Too silly!"

"And you could call it your Willy's willy. I mean . . . You may have it all to yourself, except that I need to keep it on loan, to pee."

"You are too . . . ", she murmured, head on shoulder.

"I am happy."

"Happy?"

"Are you?" he whispers.

"Am I . . . "

"Happy."

"I am . . . happy."

"If you want to give it a name you may, but—"

"Stop. I am happy. I cannot go any further, now. Not ready." She turns her face away but backs against his hip.

"Okay."

"Just okay! You are too agreeable to be believed."

"I am happy."

"You are an idiot."

"Yes. So what, then, do you call this?"

"Aah, no names. None, anyway, so silly as Willy's willy. It is me."

"Willy's willy is happy to make your acquaintance."

"Shush. Let willy rest."

"I—"

"Stop." She reaches behind to cover his mouth.

"Are you crying?"

"No. Yes. I am happy. Well. Damn, Willy. You have messed me."

"Messed?"

"Yes. It is your damned word. If I get it wrong, it is your fault."

"Yes, messed. I have fallen up a mountain into a thunderstorm. I would say 'messed' is about right."

"The sun is coming up." Thin torn blue and yellow, like a faded flag caught in a leafless tree. She stares at it and murmurs, "Winter is late."

"Yes. We should get up."

"What day is it?"

"Willy, hold my hand a minute, so." Palm to palm, tips pressed together. "Tell me, what happens now?"

"Well. Bloods mix through skin, we make love again, we go out for coffee and herring."

"No, next week, next month, next year."

"Dear Svea, let me make you another proposal."

"No, Willy, shit! May the last time be the last time!"

"Listen. Listen carefully and help me with this, because I am making it up. Now. Whatever we each want, wait. Next weekend, let's meet in a park, and not touch, and we will each tell the other what we want for next week, next month, next year. Given a whole week to think about it, as if we were free people."

"Willy, you are something. And, Willy, what am I to say if you just repeat, damnit, you want to be my father's apprentice and son-in-law?"

"I will try to be, er, original. You could just say you want to do what you are doing now, trying to straddle bug research and third world epidemics, flying six kites. I would push you to say what you want for yourself. You can ask me anything. I have less to give up; apart from you I mean."

"Where in hell did you come up with this idea, Willy? Did you have to go to a psychologist when you were a teenager too? Do you think getting in my pants makes you my key child? Go back to Uppsala and let me breathe. Maybe they, in Uppsala, will recruit you for the Greenland ice cap station, or for the CIA."

"Or something. For today it will be, umm, hard to go out the door."

"Oh, you are one big idiot, Willy!"

"Yes, and I neglected to bring my drugs. I need to get back to them before I forget your name. Err, Urðr, is it?"

"Shit, damn."

"Is that your parting benediction?"

She is thinking, in fact, *drugs*. She forgot the appointment for getting a new IUD. Never mind. Willy does not understand the outburst. Must go in soon as possible; no alarms yet.

As he goes out the door she feels a chasm open behind him. Some of herself has stuck to him and is drawn out to a thread neither can yet break. She follows him to the stairway, where he stops three stairs down and says back up at her, "We could go for a week to stay with Frans and Joost, and you could read to me from the *Book of Solomon* in Frans's old Bible, feed among the lilies. We could meet that Anna with the three kids, perhaps she would be your bridesmaid, and the one I held would be flower girl. Or we could walk along the canal, and then you could push me in and leave me to the eels and fairies and go back to the life you want." Echoing in the white shaft.

She whispers, "Willy."

He smiles, catches her eyes, which are watering, tear track across the velvet cheek. She lifts her hand just a weensy bit in a tiny wave. What a . . . Truly belongs with the fairies, a gypsy thief.

When she goes back in she finds he has left his damned *loneliness* behind, crowding the coat rack.

But as he goes clattering down the steel and concrete stairs he is thinking hard about what he must do, what he can do. Maybe that Bengt will take on an unpaid apprentice, cooking up that forge—sweeping the floor at first, of course—and four days writing the novel of P Mack and cooking PBC and martyred herrings and gathering dandelion and chive salad for her, . . . what then? Geophysics me arse.

But hear the world singing. It makes me want to say, *holy*, and use words like, OK, *chryselephantine* in a sentence, I am in the company of Paddy bloody Hannan, *gold's here men*!

***

Svea braces against the bathroom sink and stares into the mirror. Jesus what have I done, what am I doing. I should sleep now, no, of course I cannot sleep. Not the weekend amusement I told myself though I should have known, yes I did know; well what did I know? The hated furniture he called deranged-Swedish, it all got moved about, lost socks fell out, the mask on the wall is askew. Last month, this weekend, oil and water. Stupid notion of picnic-in-park that will resolve everything, good god I need to catch him and shout at him, Willy, what the hell. I called him *fool* and *idiot* but he *exalted* me, yes. Only he got the stares that once and I was afraid he was about to somehow leave before I could throw him out.

She slaps the counter and abruptly grabs pull-on wood-soled shoes, clatters down the stairs and out the front door, looks up and down the street, a shout forming in her throat, but no, she does not see him. Disappointment or relief? Who knows even which way he would have gone, meandering and asking people in the street for directions to the station. I could probably get there before him. What then? Yes let's call uncle Frans?

Breathe. Go in to office today. Mail and stuff. Be me perhaps, try. Let settle.

***

Kursverksamheten is taking its students to Stockholm—a cultural day trip—today, Willy remembers, the next day in Uppsala. I should go, he thinks, the class . . . He has a surge of affection for the class. Off he goes on the pink bike. Four buses! It is the whole Swedish language group. The classes are mixed on the busses. He finds himself with Andrei's class, but is happy to sink against the window and sleep for the half hour or so into the city. Out they hop. They are grouped and ushered a short walk to the Riksdag building, and pass, in bus-groups, across a balcony to see the lawmen doing their thing. The parliament seems very comfortable in its modern concrete curves, subtly massive on an island anchored off Old Town. At eleven thirty, the leader says, and it is passed through the bus ushers, people can take an hour for lunch and should meet back exactly here, at exactly twelve thirty (*half-one*), to board the buses again, and in the afternoon they will go to the palace. All on your own, everyone understands? Ja, ja, ja, we all know the time in Swedish now, though it is a bit odd, right, that half-one for twelve thirty?

Fair enough. Willy takes lunch at a sandwich bar, with Elsa from his class and Andrei from his hall, and they stroll about shops. Baran seems not to be here; extended honeymoon. An Englishwoman tourist stops Willy and asks for directions to the something. He pretends to understand her with difficulty and sends her two blocks this way, one north, and there you have it *altihop*!

"*Kali mera!*" adds Andrei as she expresses dubious gratitude.

At twelve thirty all board the buses and a head count is taken. Oops, one missing. It is Mahmoud from his class. At twelve forty, the usher on the bus that has waited says, We have to go, we are late. Willy says, "Okay. I will wait for Mahmoud. We will do our own thing, and we will see you back here at four thirty, right?"

General relief. Your guy, Birgit, has saved the day. Bus door hisses; brrrm.

Willy waits. There is little foot traffic, this smallish square is not exactly the beaten path, though the more or less founder of the modern nation sits there high on his green bronze horse pointing to the Riksdag across Mällaren, with a scroll rather than sword. Hey, he notices, that's that Opera House just there, behind the statue. A pedestrian comes into the square from the south, goes in front of the Opera and turns upstream along the riverfront; damn, thinks Willy, looked like the spook. What the. Leave him be, improbable and too far to chase down and besides the guy is an *asshole*. Willy stares at the corner the man vanished around and indulges a surge of distaste. Bloody bastard: *evil*. Worse than the Russians? Easier to hate because language articulates and fertilizes it, while the Russians are (were) opaque, motherless, transient thugs with whom not even the weather is arguable. And then, coming into the square following the same path as the semblance of the spook along Regeringsgatan, comes Mahmoud. At one o'oclock.

"Aaahhh," says Mahmoud, with his beatific smile, though he is really embarrassed, ashamed to some imponderable degree, that he has misheard, screwed up, and Willy has had to skip the palace to meet him. Willy reassures him, "Bet they don't even have good ice cream out there. We have the whole of Old Town to explore! In fact, I bet that Andrei and most of our class wish they were here with us! Yeah, mate!"

"Willy, there is something different about you. Is it a girl?"

Errr. Well yes; the spook is quite forgotten, and of course it was a mistaken identity.

"*Mabrouk*, Willy! Which one?" Mahmoud imagines it must be a girl from the school; his world is not so large. So, Willy gives a brief identity: sister of Rolf from my residential hall. "Well!"

"Mahmoud, *pourquoi tu ne comprends pas mon francais? Peut etre c'est trop merde simple?*"

"Wha . . . "

Oh well. Fuck the CIA, neither Mahmoud nor Baran, my brown friends, an ounce of, um, French, *my* French anyway. I'm going to start calling you Smiler the Phoenician.

They wander for a while on modern streets. There is little advertising about what is in most buildings on the outside, and Mahmoud fixes on a small graphic of bowling pins. 'What is that?' So in they go, and Willy pays for a game, and they enter a bowling alley such as Willy has seen just once in Perth, but Mahmoud never. Willy's impression of Mahmoud's exposure to the civilized world narrows. Willy coaches Mahmoud, who sails a few balls from waist level, not waiting for the mechanism to reset pins, maybe thinking he has to catch them unawares. Willy tries to demonstrate, but there is a big giggle in his heart and he does a gutter ball, then a strike, but going down onto his hands. Mahmoud then manages a ball over the gutter and into the neighboring lane, just bobbling the outside pin. Nobody playing that lane, but the players on the next-over shout. Willy grabs Mahmoud's arm, lays his head on Mahmoud's shoulder, and laughs softly, ending in a tear. Mahmoud, Mahmoud, *you are the archangel*. Mahmoud is a bit startled at this intimacy and a suggestion of tears, and steps back—Hey infidel, no weirdness!— but hangs onto his wrist. Willy thinks, should he turn up tonight at Svea's unannounced and contrary to, well . . .

So, disinvited by the eyebrows of the bowling alley staff, they go back to the street, and amble over a bridge to Gamla Stan. Arm in arm now, giggling. Willy says to himself in English, "Methinks I am a bit faint. Oh shit, off my meds five bloody days, is it?" Because he forgot this morning again in a rush. They are on a cobbled street, and they cross an arched bridge. A man in a peasant costume of perhaps one, two hundred years ago, is standing on the bridge, and winding a line onto a stick. Willy and Mahmoud stop and watch, thunderstruck.

"It is happening," says Willy. "Fit." The warmth comes over him, the premonition, but then the seizure overruns it, whoosh. Mahmoud grips his arm in alarm.

The river is an aquamarine torrent from the great lake Mällaren spilling under the narrow bridge. They, the watchers and the peasant, are alone, together. In the fairy tale heart of this city there is no-one else and no time but the peasant and the watchers. He, the peasant, pulls a golden fish, a carp as long as his arm, from the torrent, winds it up onto the bridge. The one we call Willy is gone, but the still-open eyes watch. Mahmoud goes on grasping his arm; djinns are coming and going, seizing Willy, hold onto something, four legs better than two. No sound but a low tidal vibration, and a city somewhere. And a pigeon or six.

In the time it takes the two watchers to regain verbal consciousness, the peasant has rolled the fish into a sack with his line and stick, and ambled off. Neither Willy nor Mahmoud can actually speak. They let go of each another, and stare into the river, the rush of drunken gods, at the sky, wonder where the peasant has vanished to as words come back, slower to Willy.

"Hey, what did you see there?"

"What happened to you Willy, Allahu Akbar, what happened to us?"

"Are we mad? Yes I am mad friend."

Mahmoud determines Willy is speaking gibberish and has had *un petit mal*, whatever kind of language he thinks he is speaking. He holds Willy by the shoulders, and they walk back on the bridge. Just down a side street there is a coffee house. And, determines Mahmoud from the counterperson from whom he gets two double espressos, they are near the bus pickup. And they have forty minutes.

"Mahmoud, I'm back. I had a spell. What the hell did we see back there?"

Mahmoud is unable to get more than four words in a sentence; he is disarticulated too. Well, they decide it was, anyway, just miraculous. If no supernatural agencies were involved, it was a spectacle they were privileged to see, beyond comprehension etc., bloody marvelous ("What is bloody, Willy?").

Coffee is good. It is cool, with a pleasantly dim light, in the shop.

Oopla! All of a sudden a piglet runs down the cobblestone out the door. Both see it at the same time. Mahmoud leaps to his feet and runs to the door to look, trips on the step up, and falls flat on his face in the street. Gives a cry. Willy comes up behind him just as a camera dolly rolls past, pursuing the piglet down the street. Ha!

"A movie!" says Willy to the prone Mahmoud, "and you are in it!" He helps Mahmoud to his feet, slaps him on the arm, laughs, wheezes. Mahmoud slowly recovers himself, but he has been shaken to his core once already this afternoon, and though his eyes narrow back to normal, his lips remain compressed in a frozen whoo-whaaa?

"Mahmoud, maybe the fish and the pig are in the same movie, and now us too!"

Mahmoud has upset his coffee, so they clean up a little and exchange waves and smiles with the wait people. We should stay and chat with them just to regain equilibrium, thinks Willy, but Mahmoud needs air. He has banged his forehead and knee and wants to stand and sit at the same time, to go out and to stay, in circles. So, they wander out to find the bus place across the river, back at the Opera House, and wait. Mahmoud is bobbing and muttering a bit.

"This way." Crossing the small square with equestrian statue, they link arms. The autumnal sun plays hard to get around edges of wee clouds. Willy says, "Mahmoud, *mon ami.*" Then, retreating to English, sort of editorializing, "Hey, we crashed the scene. They will edit us out or reshoot it with some strategic control of intruders. Okay, rude of me, *på svenska*, then. The filmmakers will take us out or do it all again with barricades, unless it amuses them to incorporate crossings of aliens and, how do you say, time glitches. Unless we are perhaps invisible, you know?"

"Jesus, Mahmoud, she is just over there, somewhere," gesturing southerly, "the girl. Somehow, my life . . . Where did I get the balls? If, in a couple of days, she says the magic words, then I am in the story of my life, but if she dismisses me, it is off to Novaya Zemlya. Got to send her flowers. Shit, I don't even know her address. No, not flowers. Howabout mushrooms for a princess of the fairies?

"And hey, that is that Opera House right there!" But somehow it looks like a movie set, not real; he is disequilibrated and feels as if he could fall out of time again. Look, my faint shadow bunched into a crow shape trundling over cobbestones with no feet; and then lightly snuffed out by a finger of cloud. Am I a figment of the weather? Is she real?

Mahmoud is still in a mush over the fish and piglet, and it is not obvious he is even trying to follow Willy's rant. He thinks Willy is still a bit in the grips of that whatever it was he had back there. Willy thinks, *damn*, I don't even know my own dorm phone number to call what's-his-name—What is it? Come come —Rolf, for her address. How come I did not register it?

It is not a regular bus stop, but there are a few benches, so they sit restlessly, little expostulations still bubbling from Mahmoud. And chuckles erupt from either one, like bumblebees strayed from their meadow.

Here come, shambling, a trio of what, black leather gang bangers? Stop as if they are waiting to meet someone. Long coats, oozing fuck-youse, oh and all-over makeup, eyeshadow with dark slashes. Hey, Ned Kelly and the girls. Willy presses Mahmoud's arm to get up and relinquish the bench. Don't stare at characters got up to be provocative, let the buggers take roost, and we can move about and avoid them. Loud voices, some dialect from a dark underside, incomprehensible—probably something to be glad of. Even as Mahmoud is loosing a vast smile in their direction, *hey y'all,* and stepping away, one bumps him with an elbow, with a mumbling sounding to Willy like "fucking Arab."

"Come, Mahmoud."

"Eh, your focking friend, is it? Focking friend!" "Harrh." "Is it a Palestinian d'ya think Otto?"

"Boys, I do not understand what you are saying. We are only students of textbook Swedish, waiting for a bus. Almost any bus would do. A policeman told us to take bus number nine, but we got lost, and so we parked it on the bridge there."

Mahmoud guffaws at the joke, second-hand from Eric's telling their class his tale of being charged with stealing a bus on the island of Man ("*Take bus number nine to the hostel!*"). But these buggers are not amused; they seem to be in a fug.

"Eh, it is a focking *'mericaner*?" But they are looking at Mahmoud.

"Nay, I am just a professional bastard, and my friend a contagious French leper."

Ach, wasted. A chorus of growling vilification ensues, and violet shirt steps up to Mahmoud and grabs his wrist; Mahmoud twists, but the grip tightens.

A cold chill drops over Willy like a bucket of water from a well tank. He sees himself and Mahmoud, the three oafs, a script of deadly ambush by djinns from another world dropped on him from the wings.

As if attracted to an opening of lunch-bags, an in-waddling of pigeons flashes iridescent glints on gray knuckles of a big hand reaching over this slow-moving group. An embassy of doves, not. The blink of an eye, then, instanter, the knight of the silly drills comes into Willy's knuckles. Lemme, cha. He steps forward and thrusts left hand against the elbow of the arm holding Mahmoud, then drives his other fist down on the forearm. His left fist slips up the upper arm and backhands the nose, not so hard, but feels the bone and it should bleed. Pulled it I did; sensei says don't pull the punch. Pigeons burst into flight; oaf staggers a bit in flurry.

His pals are on the other side of the bench, scrambling over it to his assistance. Willy straight punches one in the throat, harder now, and earns a gargling cry. The third is reaching in his coat. Whassat gonna be, a knife? He grabs at near coat lapel, pulls it down, and punches behind the ear—thud. Hey, so far! Violet shirt has staggered, leaving Mahmoud and coming back at Willy. The other two, each of whom he has insulted with these fists, are noisy on hands and knees. And, wait—where did this come from?—another converging on him, in denim. Breathe, shooo. Gargler on the left grabs Willy's ankle, and when he twists to kick, his right is exposed, and that new blue boy reaches long in to punch him under the ribs. Not so hard. But they stand back. There is a flash in that one's hand. They all look at it—silver with a vein of red. Willy looks too. Is it? He clenches the fists. Ready or not. All are looking at his side, gasping. Look!

Stain. Fluids are leaking out of him. Cover it with left hand, press, get somewhere. Middle of the city. Mahmoud, don't let them get you too. Mahmoud is running a circle, shouting; baddies are going in a loping cluster, supporting one another. Mahmoud has run back, knocking lagging bloody-nose Violet down. Now all gone?

Lean on bench. Time yet. Where is everybody. Not so much fluid leaking out, but ebbing. Can grief be minor furniture upon such a rapid ebbing tide? Oh, girlie, just couple miles away. Converging shades. What are they saying? Come this way, they say. *No tomorrow for you, Sonny Jim.* Aaw!

Too much sky, too much cobblestone, not enough in-between. . . blood. Yes, now it's my blood. Sit, stop pumping.

Emptying, like lantern light dimming and shrinking. Looking in from outside. What remains? Not much: Svea, a book on her chair. Someone, two, running up.

Enumerate, that's it. A counting man is a live man. Increments decreasing till vanishingly small. The limit. In. Words like a pennant run across the stage, a final word from the sponsors, composed not by his self but some arrant synapse, nor heeded by the dwindling eye upon the shrinking light. Then words gone.

He is soon gone. An ambulance is there in five minutes, before that, a staunching cloth is applied by somebody with first aid experience and a large hand, but it is gone out of him, he is imploded out of it, and now the blood gushes forth from body cavity where it has accumulated.

When the bus comes, Mahmoud is sobbing on the bench, with a medic trying to console him and a cluster of cops, one of whom steps on the bus and asks for the person in charge. Snygg Birgit immediately sees the pool of blood inside the uniformed circle of legs and no Willy, is discombobulated but takes charge, ashen.

"Mahmoud, where is Willy?" She approaches the police who surround Mahmoud on the bench, and makes it known to them that she is the leader of the bus group, of which this sobbing boy and the missing Willy were part. She is allowed to sit next to Mahmoud on the bench, takes his hand and tries to calm him. The police tacitly acknowledge this seems the only way likely to elicit any immediate intelligence about the events here.

"Mahmoud, I have to dismiss the bus, but I will stay here with you. Do you understand?"

He squeezes her hand as if it were the rail on a waterfall overlook. A policeman confers with the bus driver, and the bus departs, faces up against every window.

"I do not understand what happened. Tell them to ask others if they saw!" Mahmoud begins.

"Yes, I think they are talking to some people over there." To the policeman kneeling in front of them with notebook drawn, ready for detail that might fly off like a sparrow in a frantic flurry of pigeons, "Yes?"

Mahmoud has made several tries at a narrative and broken down sputtering. A new tack, with their revered teacher holding his hand.

"Look, it was so fast. I cannot believe it. Before, there was a very big red fish, and then a pig. Willy was very strange, and I fell and hit my head. We laughed, laughed, and came to meet the bus, and they, four of them, attack us. Why? Is it because I am African? I run. Willy did some things to them. I saw and came back. He was having the hand *so*, the blood was coming, one of them had a, yes, knife."

The kneeling policeman tells Birgit that they have apprehended two of the suspects already. Mahmoud recovers his breath and says, "Willy said, we must be in a movie, the fish and then the pig. Yes, the pig runs down the street and the people making the film after it. So we were, you know, the world was too strange. And then they attacked us, suddenly too stupid, another film, a bad one. Have they killed my friend? *They have killed our friend!*"

Birgit says to the policeman, "You will want to take him to the police station. But he needs medical attention and calming down and consolation before you will get any coherent testimony from him. If I can be with him for a little, I will call my husband to come get me there, and I would contact his people through the school."

"And the dead one? He did not have much information on him."

"Yes, I will get what the school has. I think he lives in student housing. Lived. We will have to ask his friends at the school tomorrow. You say he did not have his passport . . . You know, perhaps you could get an Arabic speaker for him, Mahmoud, but because he had this experience in learner's Swedish, shall we say, he may do better at first with me, his teacher."

***

"Svea. It's Willy."

"Willy!"

"No, it's Rolf. I mean, it's about Willy."

"So, it is him?"

'In Gustav Adolphs Torg."

"I knew it."

"What do you mean?"

"I saw some TV news in a shop. An attack on a . . . No name. He was supposed to be in Uppsala. I felt it."

"I had not seen him in days. Svea, was he with you then?"

A long quiet. Phone murmurs from the world a faint static over which Rolf cannot hear a breath, anything.

"Svea?"

"Yes?"

"Damn, Svea, he was my strange neighbor, the peanut butter chicken guy, then the odd friend, and now my crazy sister's crazy lover and, just, just, dammit?"

"Yes?"

Now she is making irregular snuffling noises, gasping. Nameless because not-named foreigner killed in Stockholm by cross-dressing gang becomes unreal Willy. Who came and . . .

"Tell me." She has had and dismissed forebodings since the TV snippet about Nameless. Now there are arrows with names on them that she cannot smash down.

"He took a tour with his Swedish class to the city, and was with an Arab classmate, waiting for the bus. The gang harassed them. Willy took them on and beat them up, but there were four of them. And one stabbed him with a knife."

"Only four!"

Rolf rides the static, sees her seeing the intruder fumbling across her life, across Rolf's too, exit stage left, as they say. Unreal. How could he possibly be erased by only four when surreal, anyway, is what she means.

"And the classmate?"

"He had cuts, broke away, got help, chased one down, something. I think the police say they have them all now, or most. Svea?"

The phone line is dreaming them into frithy silences.

"Svea, I'm coming down. I'll be there in an hour?"

But she is holding the handset to her breast with her forehead pressed to the refrigerator. She looks down the narrow hall and sees the mask is askew, touched by a gust of wind through the open window. In the small picture glass facing her on the far wall is a reflection that seems alien, and she raises the handset abruptly to confirm it is herself there. The walls of the small apartment press in as she hangs up.

"No but what is happening, merde! what has truly happened?"

She feels suddenly as if she has just dug in her pocket to give a gypsy whatever change was there, and as he disappears into the crowd she realizes her father's mother's ring, as if ever there were such a thing, was in that clutch of coins.

***

Rolf dreads going to her. The deadly silence, hell, it is the eye of a storm. When he gets there it will be shrieks and breaking of things, yes. Well, better than the silence.

***

Chapter 8

Epilogues

Adela

Dear Mrs. Mills

My son Rolf wrote to you after the death of your son Willy. Rolf had brought Willy to our home in Dalarna one weekend, and we had a very lively time of it. It was my birthday, and my daughter Svea was here, and my brother from Amsterdam. Sparks flew, and it was a grand party. By the end, Willy was part of our family. We were shattered to hear of his horrible murder.

That weekend was set alight by Willy. He was very funny, in part because of his comical Swedish, with many quaint mistakes and insertions of archaic pieces from things he was reading, and enjoying himself with them. My brother's partner, who is usually very dull, and a neighbor had hearty arguments with him about colonialism, and other things, but with much humor at Willy's way of speaking, and the men were all quite rowdy and jolly, with quite a bit of alcohol consumed. When my daughter Svea arrived, she was caught up in all of this, but even as the commotion went on, something started between her and Willy. They looked at and away from one another and started to squabble like teenagers. I believe I went to bed at about midnight, but I heard the party on and off all night, now subsiding to quiet conversation and then breaking out again in laughter and shouting. Very late, I heard a scream and doors slamming. My husband Bengt came in quite tipsy and said, Willy just asked me to be taken on as blacksmith apprentice and son-in-law. He found this very funny, and apparently everyone else did too, except for Svea.

At daylight, Rolf and Willy were on the lake in a canoe, fishing. (I think Rolf had promised the fishing to get Willy to come). By nine o'clock, Svea was making them breakfast and all were taking coffee in the smithy, my husband's work shop. It seemed there were hangovers, but the skies would clear and all could look forward to a miraculous hatch of butterflies or some such. But the high drama went on.

You should know, Svea is a difficult person, in part because she was born with a big port-wine birthmark on one side of her face, and from the first she built on it a dramatic personality, with which she bullied her whole school, even when she was the shortest person there. She was quite bright, but often defiant, and her teachers (and parents) sometimes loved her and sometimes feared her. Of course, she turned her "weapon" against everybody, including herself, and made life very difficult. For everyone. She got through school, at any rate, and was doing post-graduate study in Stockholm, on malaria. She was also studying French, to be able to work with the Red Cross or one of those new medical aid groups, and already was on their reserve lists.

Svea and Willy struck a spark, as you say it, but we did not know anything about the outcome of this before Willy was killed. Rolf says now, he was actually an intermediary and knew they had got together.

You see, I am talking about Svea now in the past tense also. Right after the earthquake in Nicaragua, and a little after Willy died, she got herself sent there in the relief effort, with emergency aid skills and also with expertise to monitor for mosquito-borne disease outbreaks with all those people out of their houses, in the open. She told Rolf she had to hurry and go. There was no time to see Bengt and me before she left; she would write and call when she could, she told him.

Now, she is dead—murdered.

I took phone calls from the Red Cross and somebody passing a message from the consular office, and, of course, the biggest Swedish newspaper and others. This narrative I have heard and been asked to repeat often already, and I cannot yet believe it. They say she confronted a looter or bandit at or near their clinic, and he (or they) slashed her with a machete. I have imagined already, many times, her challenge with her "wrath of god" pose, and the horror and fear of a superstitious native. It rips at me when a door slams or a car goes by.

But there is a new thing in the chicken house after the fox. And this I have to share with you. Without it, we would be just sympathetic friends of your son's in a faraway place. They say the autopsy shows she, Svea, was pregnant.

I am quite sure it was Willy's. I did not know she was seeing him at the time, and she had her own life I knew only in pieces, although we both lived in the city during the week and met for meals periodically. She had a significant relationship the year before that ended badly, and I knew she was still somewhat reclusive. She had not wanted "anything much to do with men" since. The child, or fetus, was just three months old. And so, you see, I believe we lost a grandchild together. Your child; then my child; and also their child.

I do not know what else I can say. It is ridiculous, of course, to say we share a grief, but there it is, impossibly heavy at both ends. I am sorry to add to the burden, but I think you would want to know.

I may be able to write more when it settles a bit with me, and answer such questions you might have. Just now we are shattered.

My most sincere condolences,

Adela Bergström

* * *

Svea's Journal Pages

There are a few crumpled pages torn out of a Panamanian school notebook, smoothed and inserted behind the cover sheet. Rolf flips through to check for other entries, and a few folded pages in the back fall out. Svea's pages are in Swedish and English mélange, aggressively scrawled in ballpoint. The folded pages are a crayon-illustrated rendering of "Waltzing Matilda", evidently by Willy, Rolf surmises. "This is my folk," Rolf hears Willy say.

The program field director recommended keeping a personal journal. Said I have never wanted to look in a mirror, piss off. He says, of course there is the shift log, but most people "benefit" (miming the quotes with his fingers) from anchoring themselves with personal diaries, regardless of how they say these appear to them in the future; that the recorded voice of the past is a bridge. Did not respond, so he repeated it. Piss off, I wanted to repeat.

Be careful: he has the power to send me back.

Willy, I say:

> You named all the parts of my body, Gudrun, Tess, Flapper, Gildedstern (I think), who could remember, certainly not you, your memory was a grab of sand, it seemed, so renaming:
>
> My blaze was Rioja, after a Tinto that we drank, from demonic coat of arms gentled to a toast; Oh.
>
> My old armor does not fit over Gildedstern and Flapper

173

and all the rest
Clumsy am I with all these named and name-forgotten
parts declining to articulate
Fluids leak out of my orifices, shit piss damn

Madman slaughtered cremated dispatched and dispersed
as gases
Will he, Willy, come back on the breeze, crawl up my nose
Perhaps until that old domesticity that others like Taavi
achieve with this world

Here I am, where the earth shook, the poor die, and the
rich steal the aid, the drugs.
I do not think I will endure unto that domesticity.

But Willy I think, no I know I am pregnant.

Should I go and find and tell your mother? Then I could go and tell
my mother. Mothers.

A damned child. I surprise myself saying 'child', as if I might. Willy,
we were both too mad to be parents. You with your bungling
Myshkin innocence. Me: I had closed the door on fairyhood and
gone with clenched jaw into unsentimental education. I opened
the door out of curiosity and you took it off the hinges. Now I am
a carcass. The sarcasm looks down at the carcass, sees itself as shit
in the ruins of an earthquake.

You said, Willy, I only wonder if it was you with your blue-black hair
that blew out of the tallest tree in the broadest forest, and here you
are, you said. Who else would have dared to utter Swedish nursery
rhymes against me but a child? Ridiculous immigrant. My defenses
were in all the wrong places; and they all watched me crumple like
the bull that is two children under a blanket at a garden party.

Willy, I said once, where does this *tenderness* come from, is it part
of your idiocy. Then you said, I thought it was from you. And so, it
is like a couple walking on a strand, wondering whose footprints

those might be, then realizing they are their own. But then the violence you did upon those boys. Who killed you.

You *liked* to mock yourself in mangled Swedish, in part a comedian, but in larger part self-doubting, which was disarming. Idiot immigrant, not long enough to be mine, and yet. Once you said, in English, I would love . . . and froze there, as if I had stopped you. Yes, I stopped you, and you were silent, gone into what drift, and I said, Willy are you having a "fuzzy bit", and you squeezed my hand and whispered, *no.*

Willy, you were cracked all over and your madness shone through. You said my birthmark was not a shield, it was only a grille over a portal, and I let you touch me there with your fingertips. Damn it, Willy. After all the comings and goings of that weekend, I think that was the moment my womb cracked.

Let me eat with the orphans, I asked once. So I did. They stared at me, they also with blue-black hair and black eyes, but chocolate skin. Perhaps they are afraid of me, marked by Satan, or uncertain anyhow. Some sat close and stared at my blaze. I thought, maybe it will draw them a little out of their shock and losses, seeing I do not demand smiles, might we be friends in calamity for a glance or a brush of hands, oh they are too somber. Fatalistically glazing over in the small aftershock I felt, except for a few quiet sobs from bottoms of throats from, as it were, designated weepers. Let us all cry together, I thought.

***

once a jolly swagman
camped by a billabong
under the shade of a coolibah tree -
and he laughed and he sang
as he waited till his billy boiled,
You'll come a Waltzing Matilda
with me.

down came a jumbuck
          to drink at the billabong.

up jumped the swagman
          and gobbled him with glee -
and he sang as he stuffed that
          jumbuck in his tuckerbag
You'll come a Waltzing Matilda
          with me

down came the squatter
    mounted on his thoroughbred.
down came the troopers -
    one, two, three.
whose is the jumbuck
    you've got in your tuckerbag
You'll come a Waltzing
    Matilda with me

up jumped the swagman
dived into the billabong,
you'll never take me alive, said he!

—now his ghost may be heard
as you walk down by that billabong
You'll come a waltzing matilda with me.

Glossary

Banjo Patterson:	*National poet of 19th century Australia, notably of "Waltzing Matilda"*
billabong:	*a water hole in a seasonal river bed*
billy:	*thin pot with wire handle and lid, used to make tea over camp fire*
bulldust:	*fine red or white dust, often deep on outback roads*
caliche:	*a calcium carbonate cemented soil pan*
corroboree:	*Aboriginal get-together*
eh?	*common interjection in countries of the former British Commonwealth (and elsewhere); typically a rhythmic use like "bloody", as in up the bloody creek, eh?*
Falu red:	*a dark red paint pigmented by hematite, originally from Falun district copper mines*
Farmor:	*father's mother – ie paternal grandmother*

goanna: any species of large Australian lizard, from 2-ft racer to 8-ft bungerra

gossar: lads

key child: children with their own house keys on the streets between school and parents getting home from work were a national anxiety

Linné: Linnaeus promulgated classification of species, and was thus a forerunner of Darwin. The Hotel Linné in Uppsala was demolished in 2018.

P Mack: The photo of the grave marker of P Mack was taken by Geoff Smith d 1996. The entry on P Mack in WA Lonely Graves, by Kevin and Yvonne Coate (Hesperian) says Mack was:
"a prospector and trail blazer, who was attacked by natives on 14 July 1894, and died 3 days later. Phil Mack and his mate Sunshine Fowler from western New South Wales came to the west to find gold... They pulled up to camp at the rocks where Mack met his death. It is said he was kneeling making a damper,

*with seemingly friendly natives looking
on, but they were Wall-eye Joe, famed
for his cunning and his two gins. One of
the women engaged Mack's attention
drawing lines on the ground to indicate
the whereabouts of water. The man had
found their small axe used to cut tent
pegs and dragging it along with his toes,
struck Mack over the head. Sunshine
rushed to his assistance and received
a blow on his hand nearly severing his
fingers. There was another party of
men camped nearby and shouts quickly
brought assistance, but it was too late for
poor Mack."*

Morsdottir, dottirsmor: Mother's daughter, daughter's mother; a
parody of old Norse naming

mulga: a scrubby desert tree (acacia); also,
mulga-dominated terrain (or just "bush")

Ned Kelly and the girls: Ned Kelly was an Australian outlaw and
horse thief whose forbears, some
claimed, were cross-dressing Fenians

näck: Scandinavian fairy, water spirit

Nova (Novaya) Zemlya: Russian Arctic island above latitude 70 N

Pissed as a newt:	*drunk as a skunk, etc*
possie:	*spot, location (from ANZAC abbreviation of army field position*
Swandry:	*a New Zealand felted wool bush overshirt*
student nations:	*at Uppsala University, social institutions loosely based on regional origins*
tropo:	*heat-demented; "bonkers"*
quartz and laterite float:	*quartz and iron oxide pebbles lying on surface*
ute:	*Australian two-door vehicle on car chassis ("utility"), typically a ranch runabout*
Vegemite:	*An Australasian yeast extract spread detested by the rest of the world*
Waitakere Range:	*a low range near Auckland, New Zealand*
Yngve Frey:	*A book titled "Who loves Yngve Frey" by Claeson tells of a farm bondsman who regrets nobody knows what the handle to a scythe is called, anymore; made into movie 1973*

Sources

Page viii   Song Credit: Girl in Tree - Fritz Sjöström, 1955. Permission granted by heirs of the lyricist

Page 7   Photo credit: Geoff Smith (deceased). Permission granted by Yvonne and Kevin Coate, authors of West Australian Lonely Graves

Page 40   Photo credit: Terry Gulliver

Page 45   Photo credit: Terry Gulliver

Page 162   Photo credit: Terry Gulliver